121

1967

1977

First edition 2021

Library of Congress Catalog Card Number pending
ISBN 978-1-5362-0762-0 (hardcover)
ISBN 978-1-5362-0763-7 (paperback)

20 21 22 23 24 25 CCP 10 9 8 7 6 5 4 3 2 1

Printed in Shenzhen, Guangdong, China

This book was typeset in Scribbles AF and hand-lettered by the author-illustrator.
The illustrations were done digitally except the characters' artwork,
which was done in traditional media.

Walker Books US
a division of
Candlewick Press
99 Dover Street
Somerville, Massachusetts 02144

www.walkerbooksus.com

Sylvie

Sylvie Kantorovitz

Walker Books

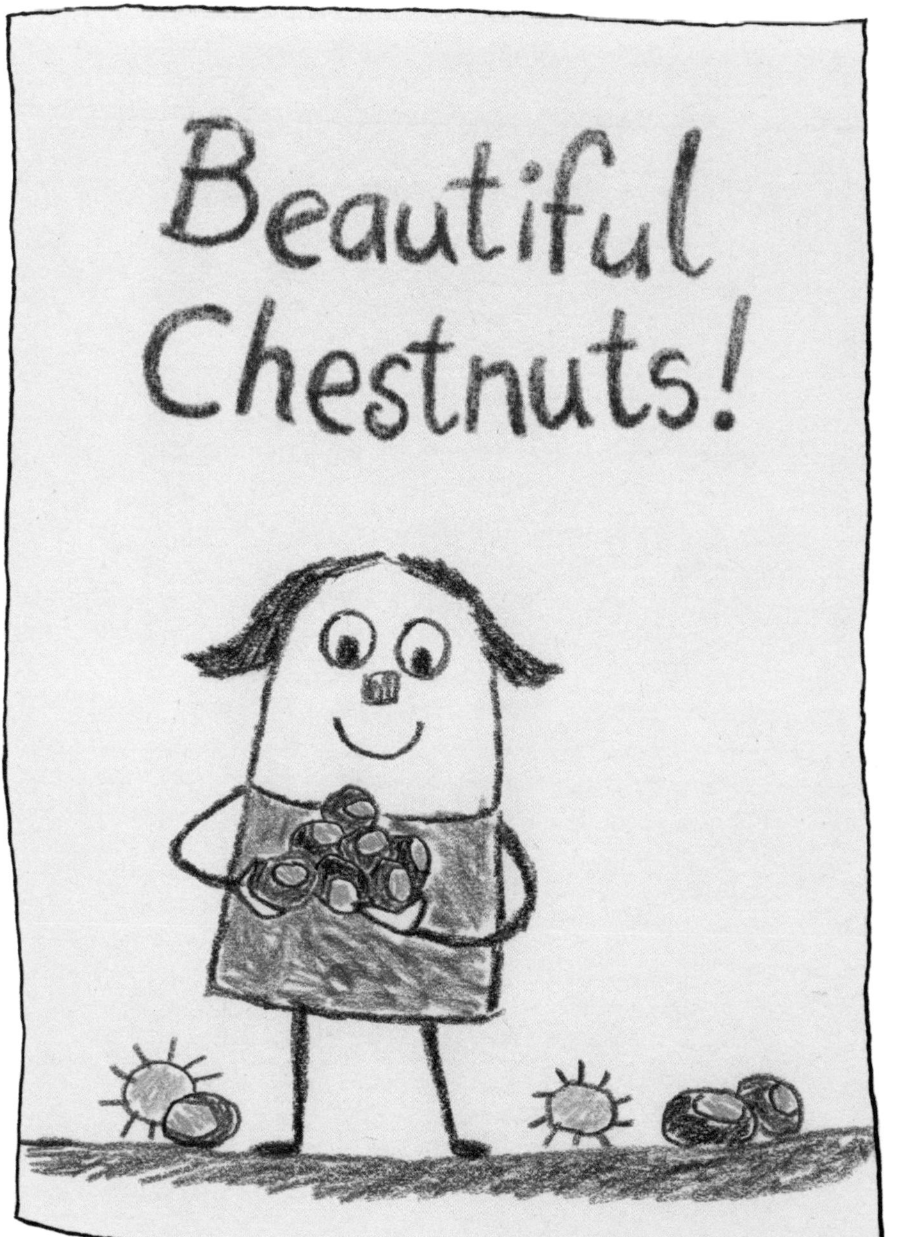
Beautiful Chestnuts!

I was born in Morocco. When I was five, my parents left their country to settle permanently in France.

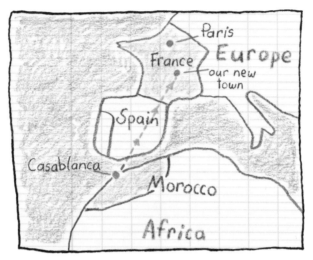

In France, we lived in a school.

It was called a Boys' Normal School.

It was a small college where students earned an elementary-school teaching degree.

My father had just been made school principal . . .

*Principal

and our apartment was on the second floor,

at the end of a long hallway of classrooms.

My own school was not far.
I walked there and back.

In the afternoons, Mom would already be home
from the school where she taught fourth grade.

After a quick snack, there was always
a lot of homework.

We loved the two chestnut trees
in the front courtyard.

The challenge was to go around and around
without ever touching the ground.

But drawing was what I really loved to do.
More than anything!

The chestnuts—or *marrons*—were not edible.
But they were oh-so beautiful.
Like freshly varnished wood.

Once, at the park, we saw a man
carving a chestnut with a pocketknife.

And he gave it to me!

True to form, Alibert wanted what I had.

On the way home, there was a boy.

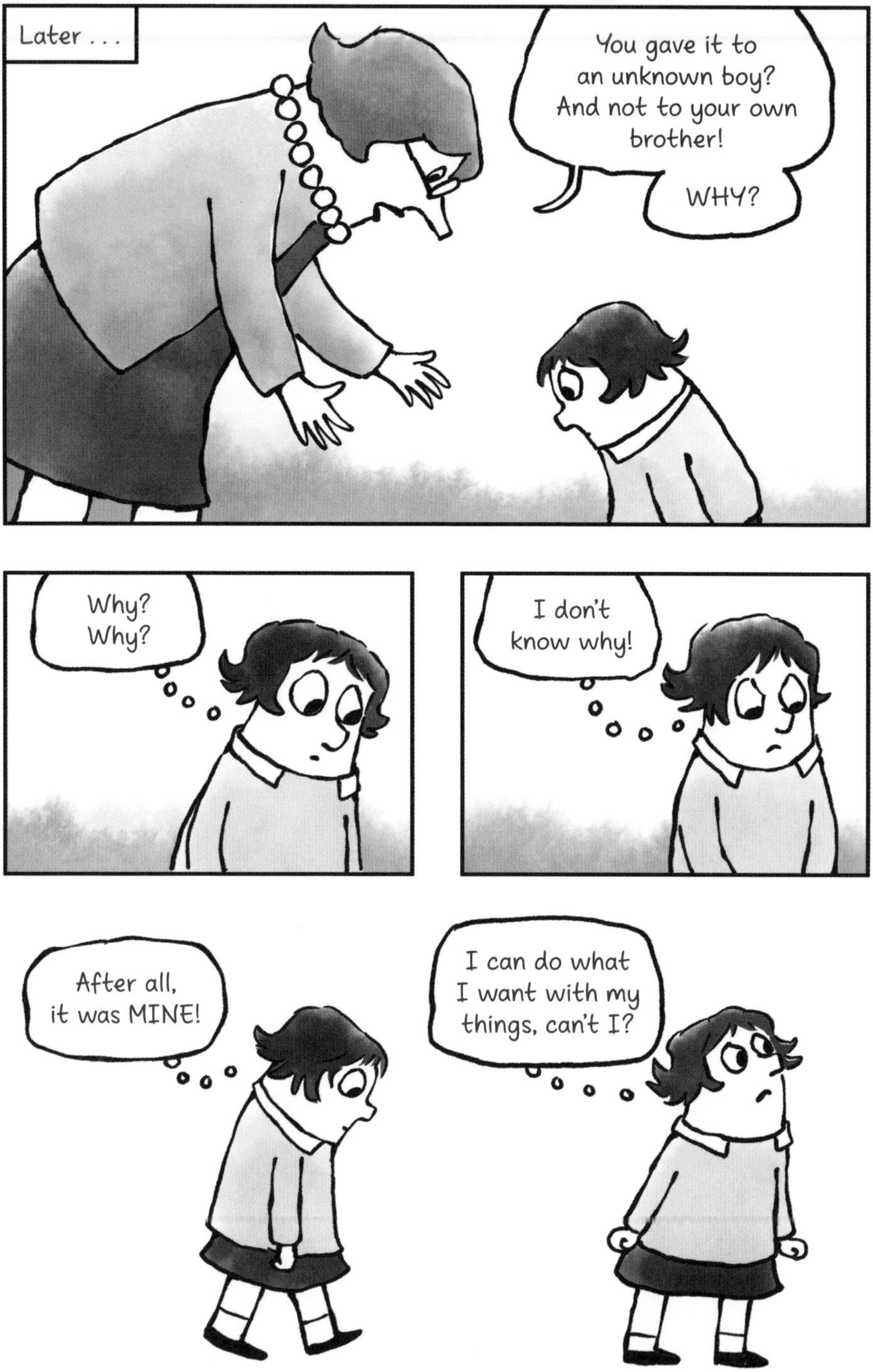
Later . . .
You gave it to an unknown boy? And not to your own brother!
WHY?
Why? Why?
I don't know why!
After all, it was MINE!
I can do what I want with my things, can't I?

Later, when I had my
own pocketknife, I tried
to carve chestnuts
into little baskets.
They never looked perfect
like the one I gave away.

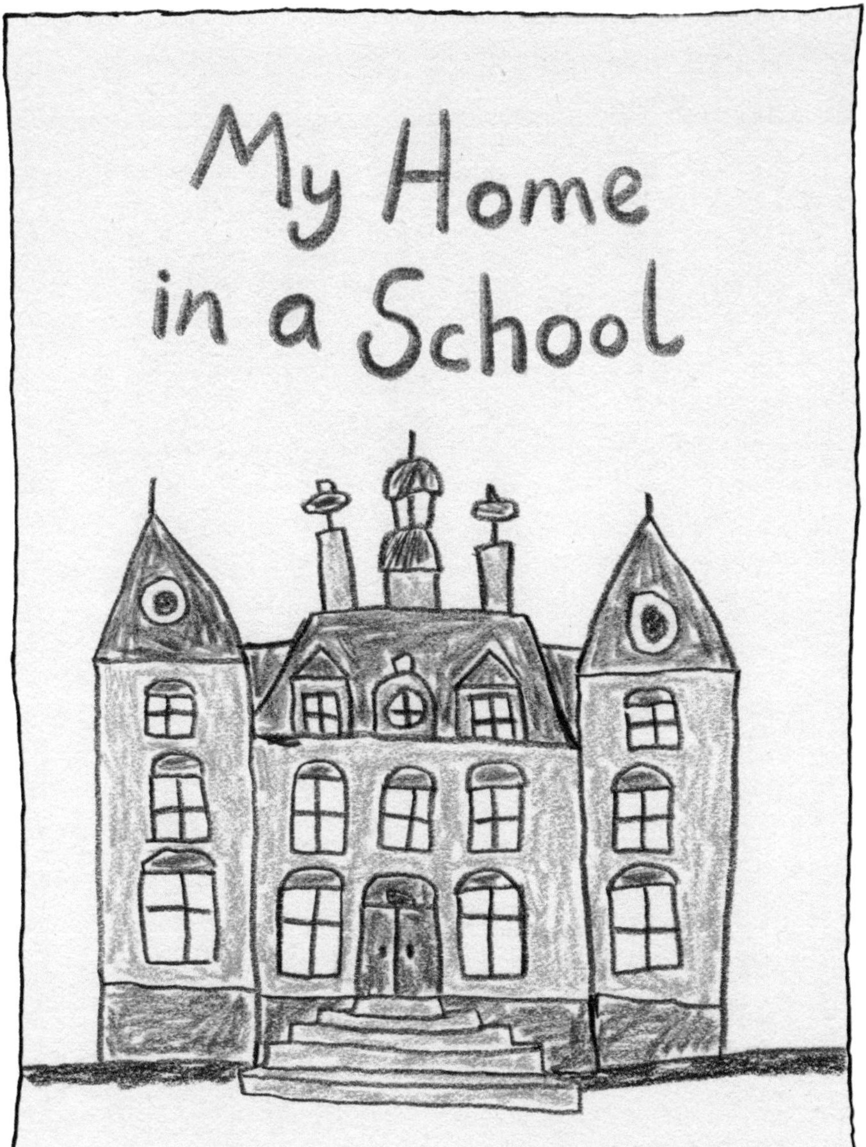
My Home
in a School

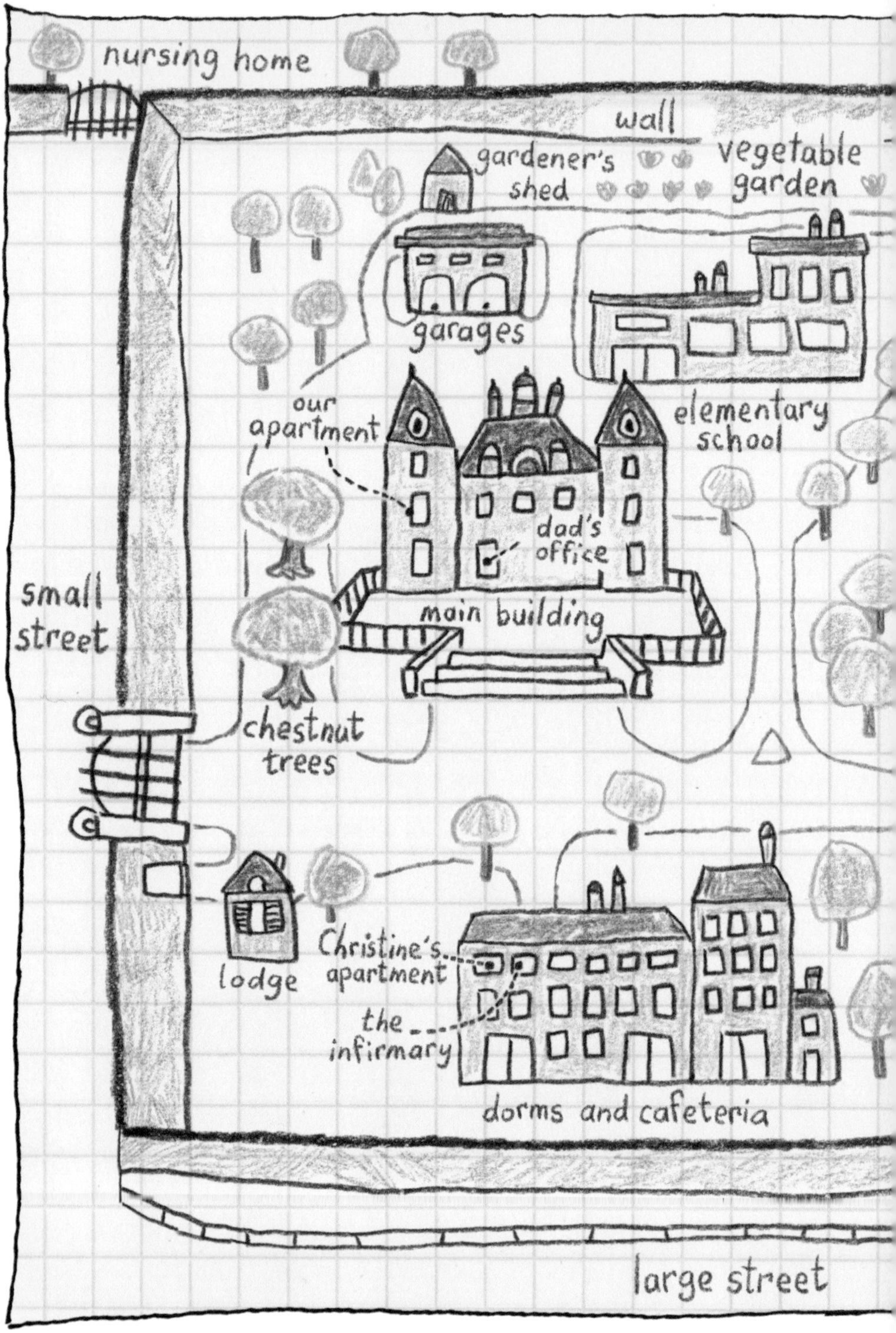
nursing home
wall
gardener's shed
vegetable garden
garages
our apartment
elementary school
dad's office
main building
small street
chestnut trees
lodge
Christine's apartment
the infirmary
dorms and cafeteria
large street

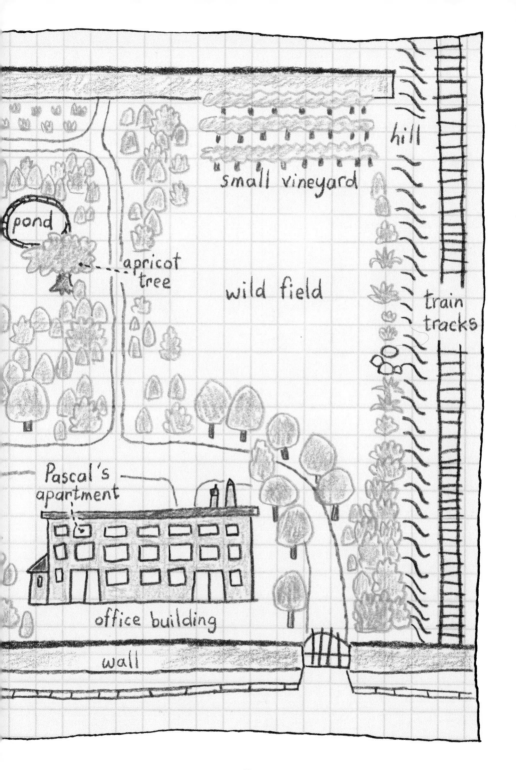

hill

small vineyard

pond

apricot tree

wild field

train tracks

Pascal's apartment

office building

wall

The school was a fantastic playground.

* *Ciel* = Sky/Heaven
* *Enfer* = Hell
* *Terre* = Earth

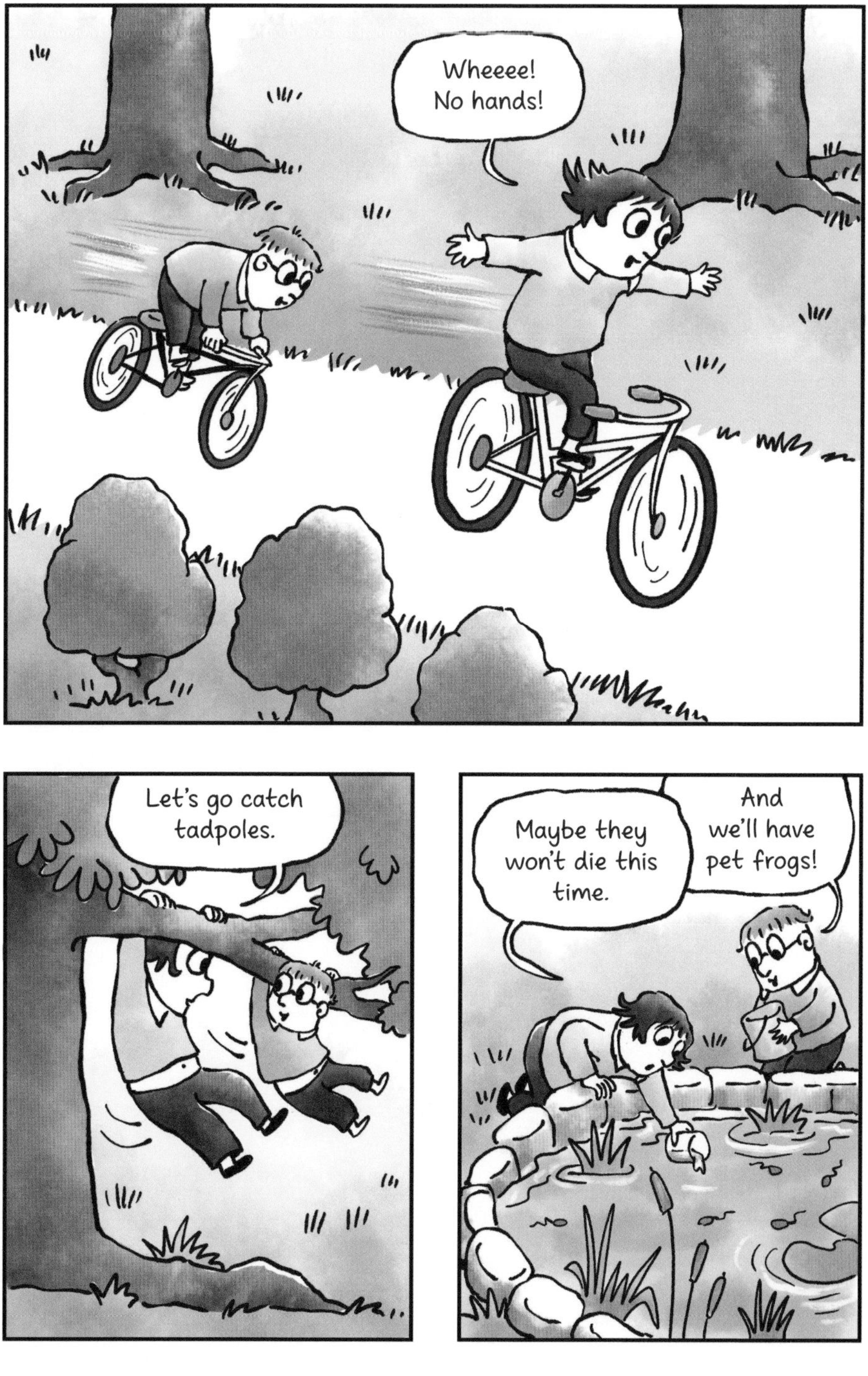
Wheeee!
No hands!
Let's go catch tadpoles.
Maybe they won't die this time.
And we'll have pet frogs!

We barely noticed the students and faculty.
They belonged to their boring world.

But we did befriend Madame Laporte,
the caretaker who lived in the lodge . . .

and Mademoiselle Petit,
our father's secretary.

There was also Monsieur Vieublé, the gardener.

Monsieur Vieublé was not fond of kids.
We kept our distance. He kept his.
Which made him incredibly mysterious.

We spied on him with relish.

Once, we found our way to his underground lair.
It was all tools and plant things.

No skeleton, no treasure. But what a thrill!

Let's go now. Before he comes back.

Luckily, we weren't the only children living there. The school came with two built-in friends:

Pascal, the son of the treasurer,

and Christine, the daughter of the school nurse.

We just had to go downstairs, and one or both of them would often join us.

Sylvie, Alibert, I want to show you a new trick!

Hey, guys, let's play tag!

Sometimes we played house in the bushes,
where we would bring scavenged food . . .

and munch on the tips of clover flowers.

Gently
pull the petals
out.

Then gnaw
on the tips.

Wow!
It's sweet!

Sometimes we waved at the passing trains,
counted the cars, and made up stories.

The passengers blurred past us,
anonymous and mysterious.

Who were they?
Where were they going?

There was a song on the radio.

*Où va-t-il ce train qui siffle
dans le silence
de la nuit?*

*Where is it going,
that train that whistles in
the silence of the night?

That line filled me
with longing. I wasn't
even sure why.
But I wanted to be on
that train too.

With Christine, we also loved to play teacher
in the classrooms by the apartment.

Which really meant free use of
the blackboard.

Occasionally, we would visit Monsieur Vuillard,
the biology professor.

Let's go see what's
new with Monsieur
Vuillard.

His domain was full of wonders,
some of them deliciously creepy.

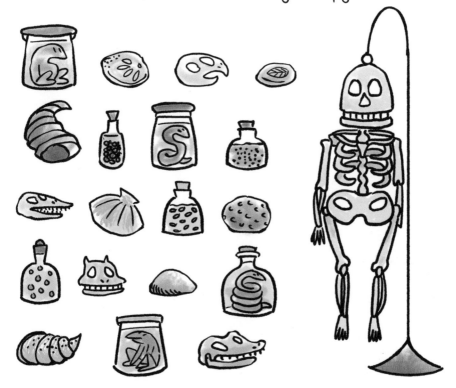

He was passionate about nature preservation.

He was the first person I ever heard talk about the responsibility of each person toward our world.

His convictions were contagious.

Pascal's grandmother lived on a farm nearby.
He knew so much about animals and even first aid!

Once, Alibert got a splinter in his knee.

At some point, however, playing with him became uncomfortable.

I started to make up excuses.

I always loved seeing Christine.

I wrote about her
in my private
notebook.

I didn't want to be a doctor, though.

At school,
Mademoiselle Jolie,
our teacher,
asked:

I was the only one without a plan for the future.
Was something wrong with me?

I wasn't thinking about the future.
I just wanted to stay forever in the
safe world of my home and family.

One rainy day, going through barely used
doors and up flights of stairs, Christine and I
arrived under the eaves of the main building.

We had discovered where the school
stored things that were no longer needed.

Christine left with her loot, and I tackled mine.

Poupinet was the local stationery store,
where my parents had a running tab and where
I was allowed an occasional purchase.

How beautiful I made
my attic treasures!

My absolute favorite spot in the whole school was the little storage room behind my dad's office.

It was always well stocked with paper, pens and pencils, tape and paper clips, erasers and markers.

The rules were simple. If Dad had a visitor, I had to be very quiet.

If he was alone, I could interrupt.

I loved it when my dad called me Sylvette!
It made me feel so loved.

My dad knew so much!
Would I know that much one day?

Also stored in the back room were two of his prized possessions: the portable typewriter he bought as a young man . . .

and his *Larousse Encyclopedia* in six volumes.

I spent hours in this quiet little room.

The encyclopedia's illustrations were a constant source of inspiration. I drew from my favorite color plates: animals, flags, and traditional costumes.

There was so much in these six volumes!
So many facts! So much wisdom!

How can they know every fact and date and place and famous person?

The logo filled me with wonder: the Larousse goddess generously spreading the seeds of knowledge over the world.

Je sème à tout vent

I sow to all winds

My dad was like her with his students! Spreading his knowledge!

Eventually his students would spread **their** knowledge to **their** students.

At one point, I thought I would read every single entry in the encyclopedia.

That plan, however, was short-lived.

But I never got tired of looking at the pictures.

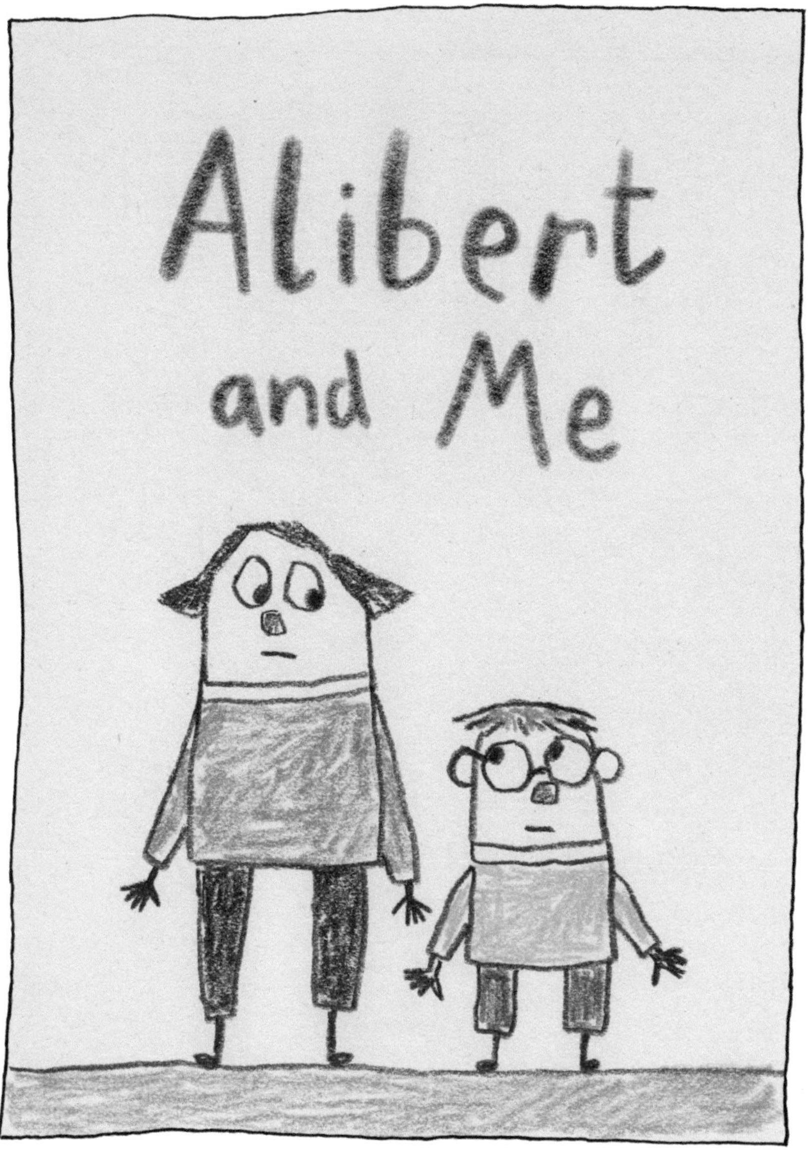
Alibert and Me

For years, Alibert and I shared a bedroom.

We played a lot together.

The trouble was, he always wanted to join in when I was playing with friends.

Alibert, leave us alone!

Sylvie, you MUST include your brother!

He should play with HIS friends.

But Alibert didn't have friends.
I believed it had to do with his name.

What were our parents thinking? Really!

Good thing MY name doesn't rhyme with a stinky cheese!

At school he was teased a lot.

Ali-bert Camem-bert   Ali-bert Camem-bert

Once, on the playground, some kids
started pushing him around.

Annoying or not, Alibert was **my** brother.

I was ready to fight.

Alibert had no trouble fighting with **me**!

Every single day, we would get into a fight.

ENOUGH!

You two behave like animals!

She started it!

He started it!

Mom was at her wits' end.

I do NOT want to hear who started it!

How I wished I were an only child.

Alibert and I were not the only ones fighting: our parents did not always get along.

Their arguing could get loud.

Sometimes a terrifying word would be uttered.

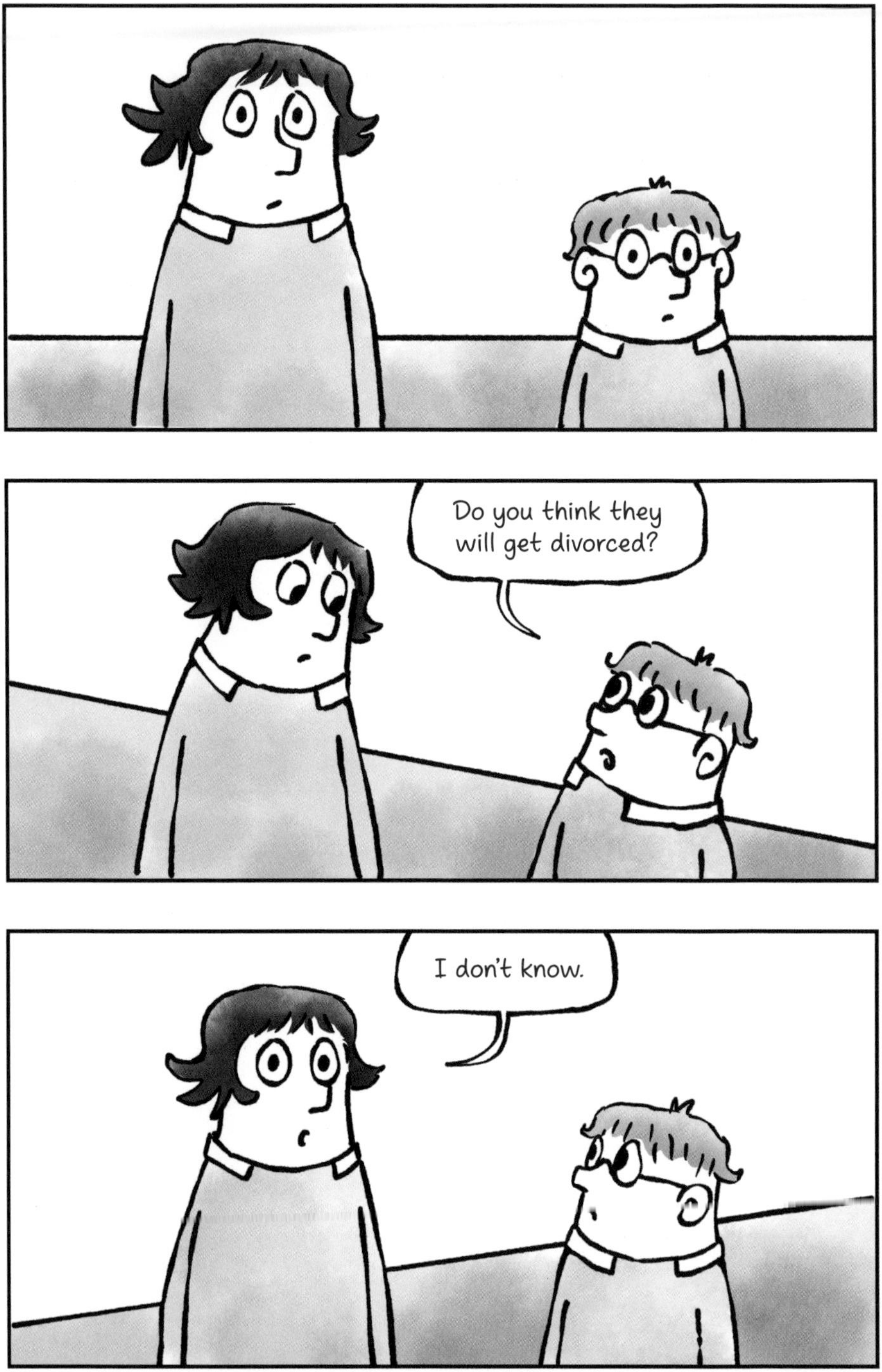
Do you think they will get divorced?
I don't know.

Sometimes it could get dramatic!

And the fights always ended
with our mother in tears.

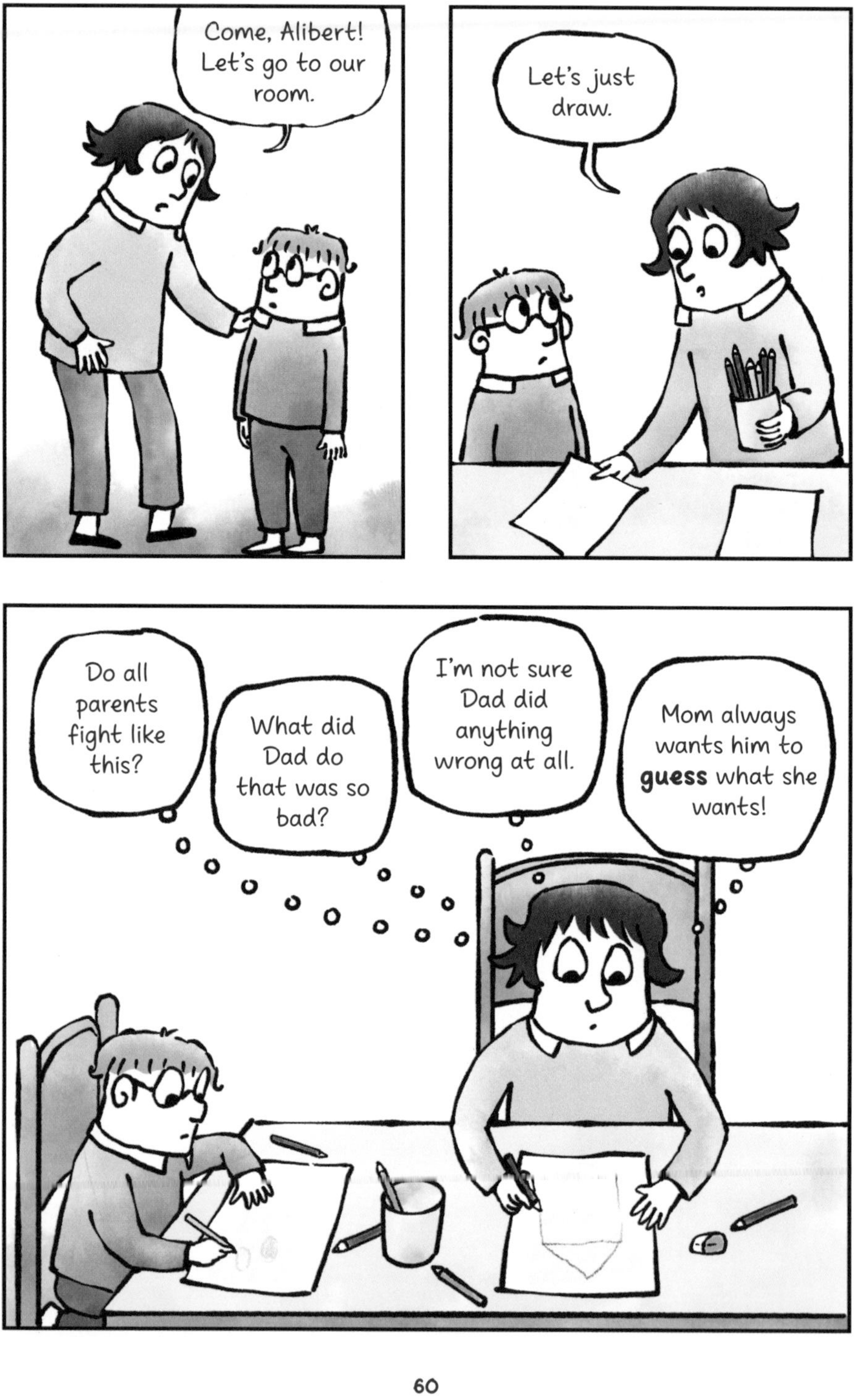
Come, Alibert! Let's go to our room.
Let's just draw.
Do all parents fight like this?
What did Dad do that was so bad?
I'm not sure Dad did anything wrong at all.
Mom always wants him to **guess** what she wants!

I really wished they got along.

Sometimes our aunt Flora would
come and visit for a few days.

She always brought wonderful presents.

One year, she brought two beautiful sets:
one of paints and one of markers.

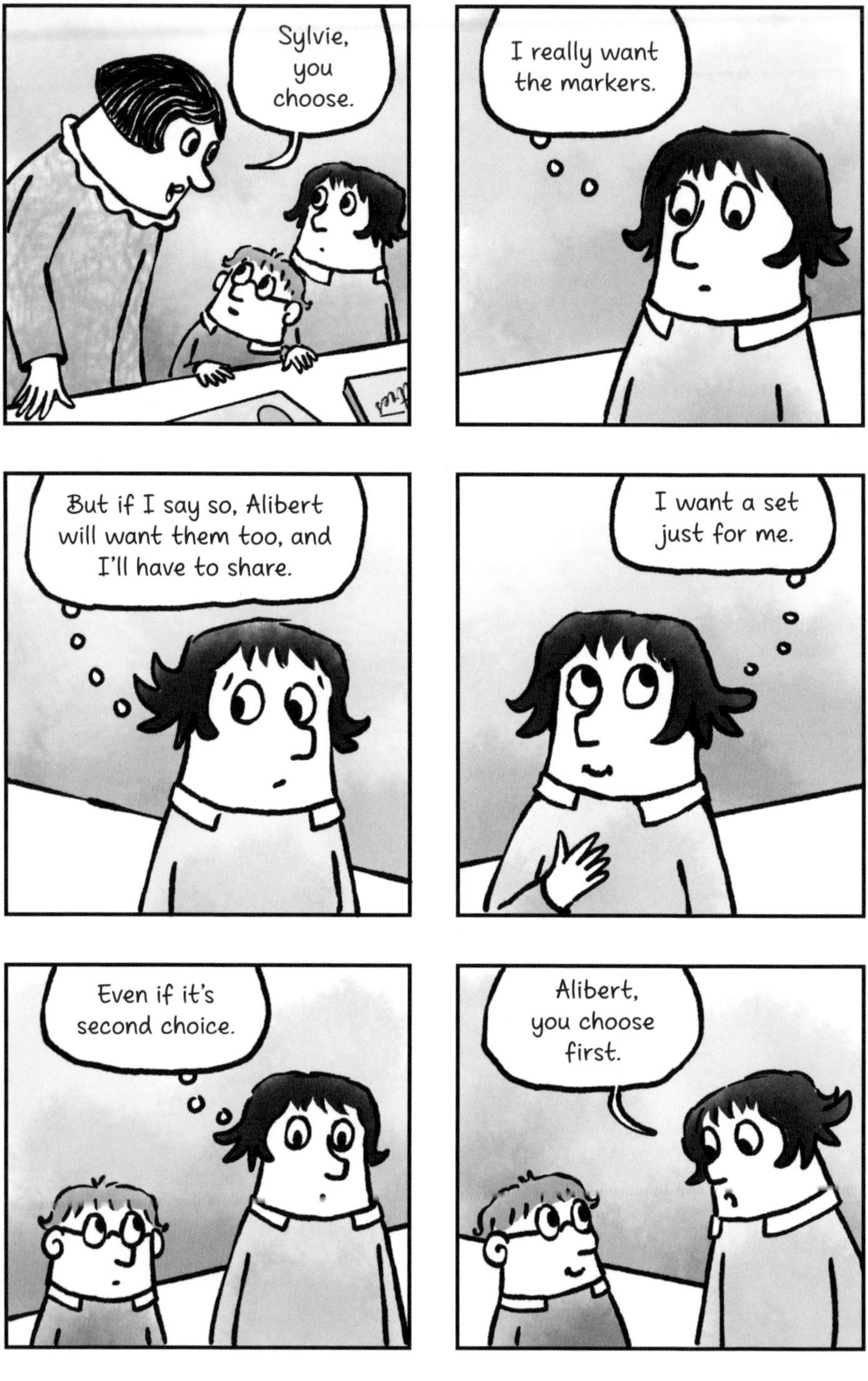
Sylvie, you choose.
I really want the markers.
But if I say so, Alibert will want them too, and I'll have to share.
I want a set just for me.
Even if it's second choice.
Alibert, you choose first.

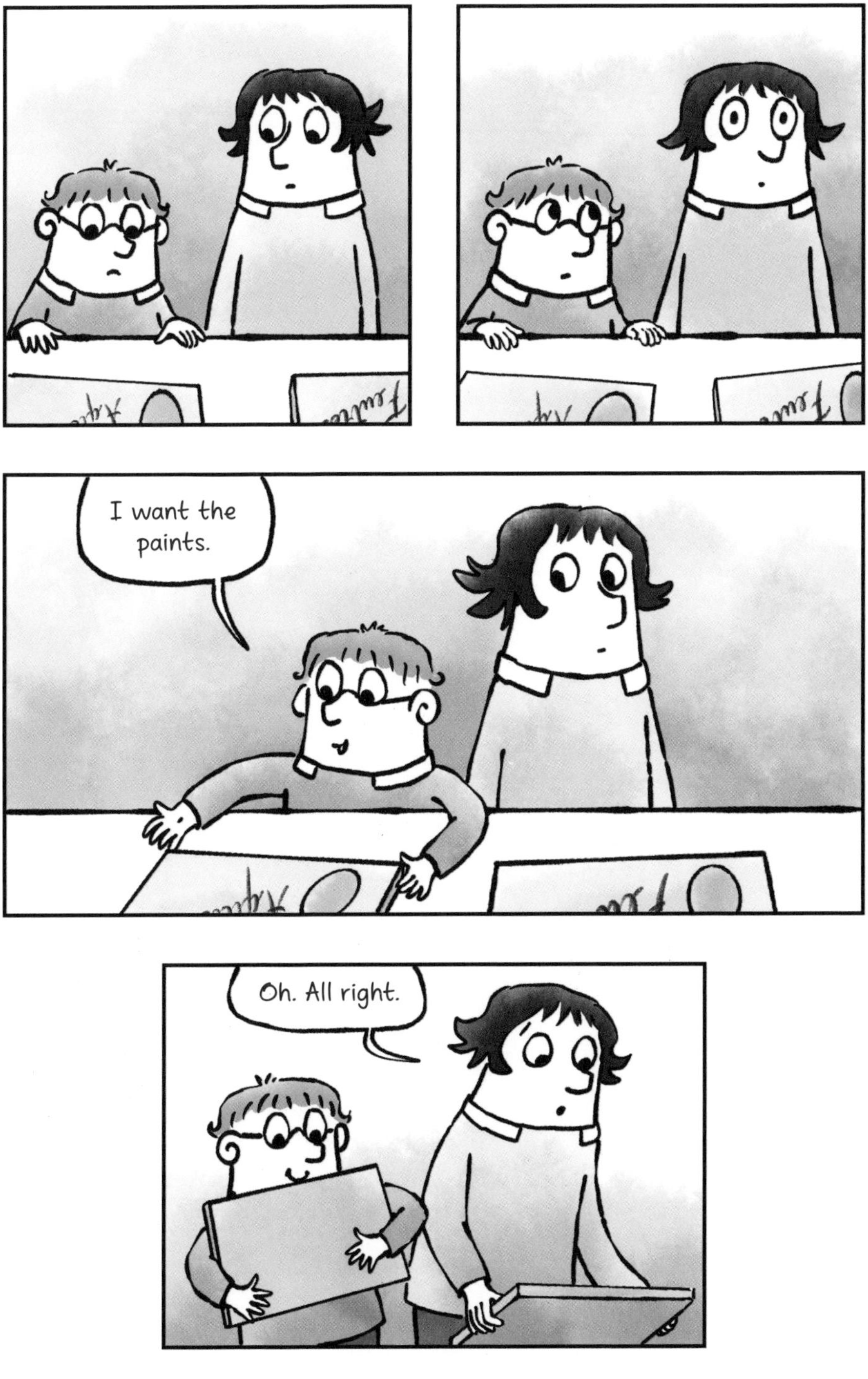
I want the paints.
Oh. All right.

I knew not to show
any emotion,
but this is how
I felt inside.

We didn't love Aunt
Flora only for the
presents.

She also brought joy, laughter,
and singing along with her.

We really wanted to do what she asked.

And yet we kept fighting,
long after Aunt Flora left . . .

until once, shortly after my eighth birthday,
when it suddenly didn't seem worth it anymore.

And we
stopped . . .

just like that.

We barely ever fought again.
But we rarely played
together either.

I Don't Want to Be Different

Sometimes at school I had to mention
that I was not born in France.

I was born in Marseille!

I was born in Lyon!

I was born at the Villette's hospital!

Don't ask me! Please don't ask me!

And you, Sylvie, where were you born?

I was born in Casablanca, in Morocco.

*Black-Foot (or *Pied-Noir*) was used as a pejorative term for French people born in North African countries.

Oh, how I wished I was born in France like all the others!

73

And then there was my family's religion: we were Jewish. Alibert and I were the only Jewish kids in our entire school.

All the others went to church on Sundays. I was different. And I didn't want to be different!

Whenever possible, I let people assume I was like them.

Occasionally there were painful comments:

Another time:

I had to ask my dad.

And still another time:

This time I didn't have to ask my dad.

Why? Why did people say mean things like that?

Mom's advice was a bit confusing:

I felt like I was going through life with a secret shame. And I was in terror of being found out.

And yet I felt loyal to my religion. I never lied about it. It would have felt so wrong!

Jesus was a very good man! A wise man!

The thing is, his followers believe he was the son of God.

And we Jews do not believe that.

Ooooh!

Well, if that was the main difference, it didn't seem like a big deal to me.

Life would be a lot easier without all these different religions!

After all, the important thing is to be a good person, isn't it?

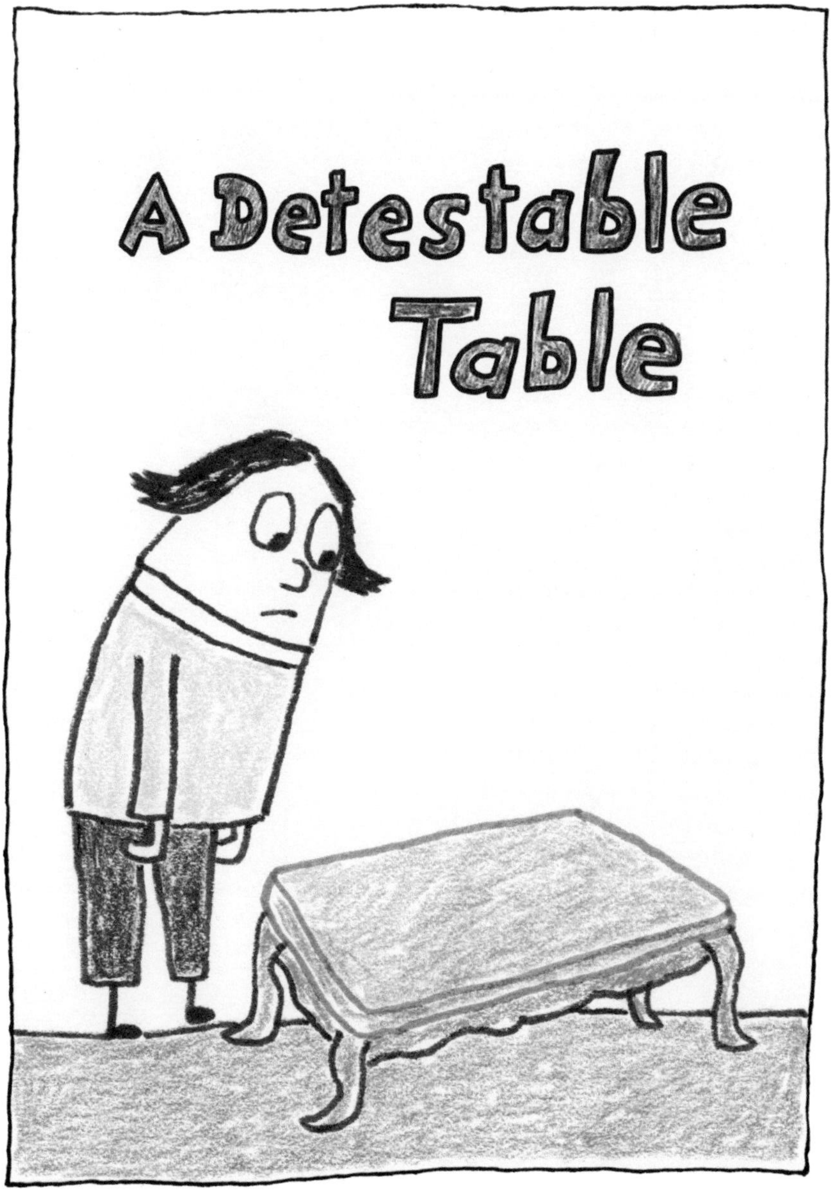
A Detestable
Table

One year, my parents redecorated the apartment.

They liked fancy stuff with a lot of carving and gold trim.

There was the sofa with
matching armchairs.

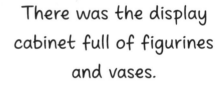

There was the
mirror-and-shelf set.

There was the display
cabinet full of figurines
and vases.

This was not furniture to my liking.
Mainly because I had to polish it regularly.

There were also various oriental carpets,
one of them in the dining room, where we
had lunch on Sundays.

After our meal, I had to brush every single crumb off the carpet.

Apparently the carpet fibers were more valuable than my free time!

And then there was the living room table!
It had a fancy top made of onyx.

On the table sat
a crystal ashtray,
heavy as a boulder.

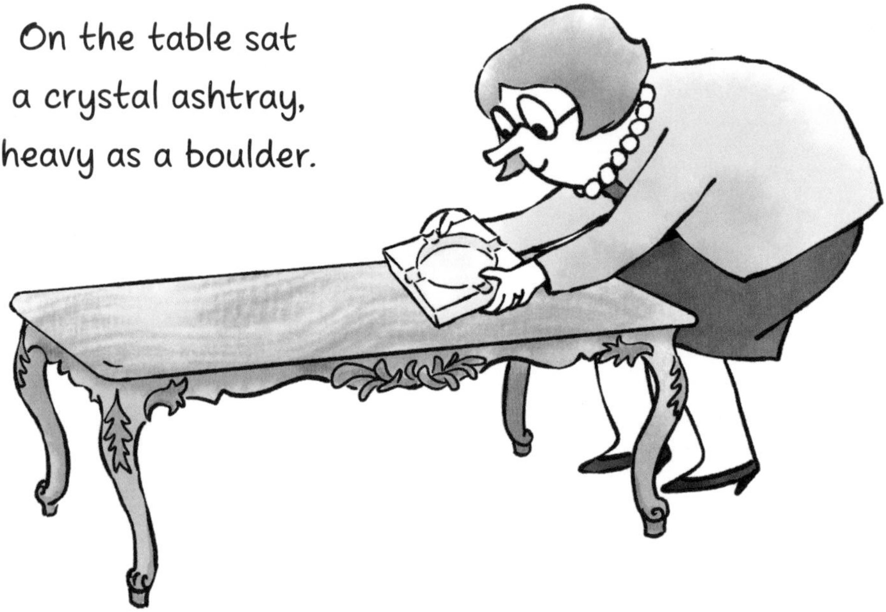

Once, I was drawing at the table . . .

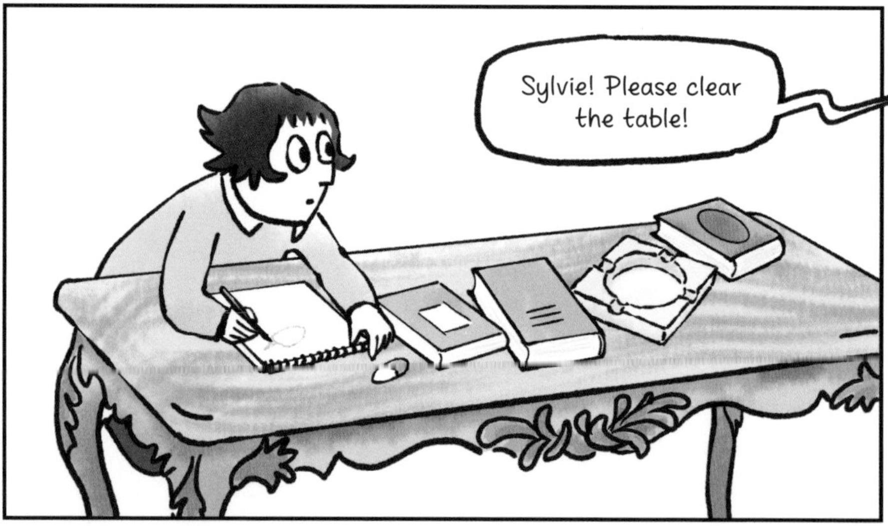
Sylvie! Please clear the table!

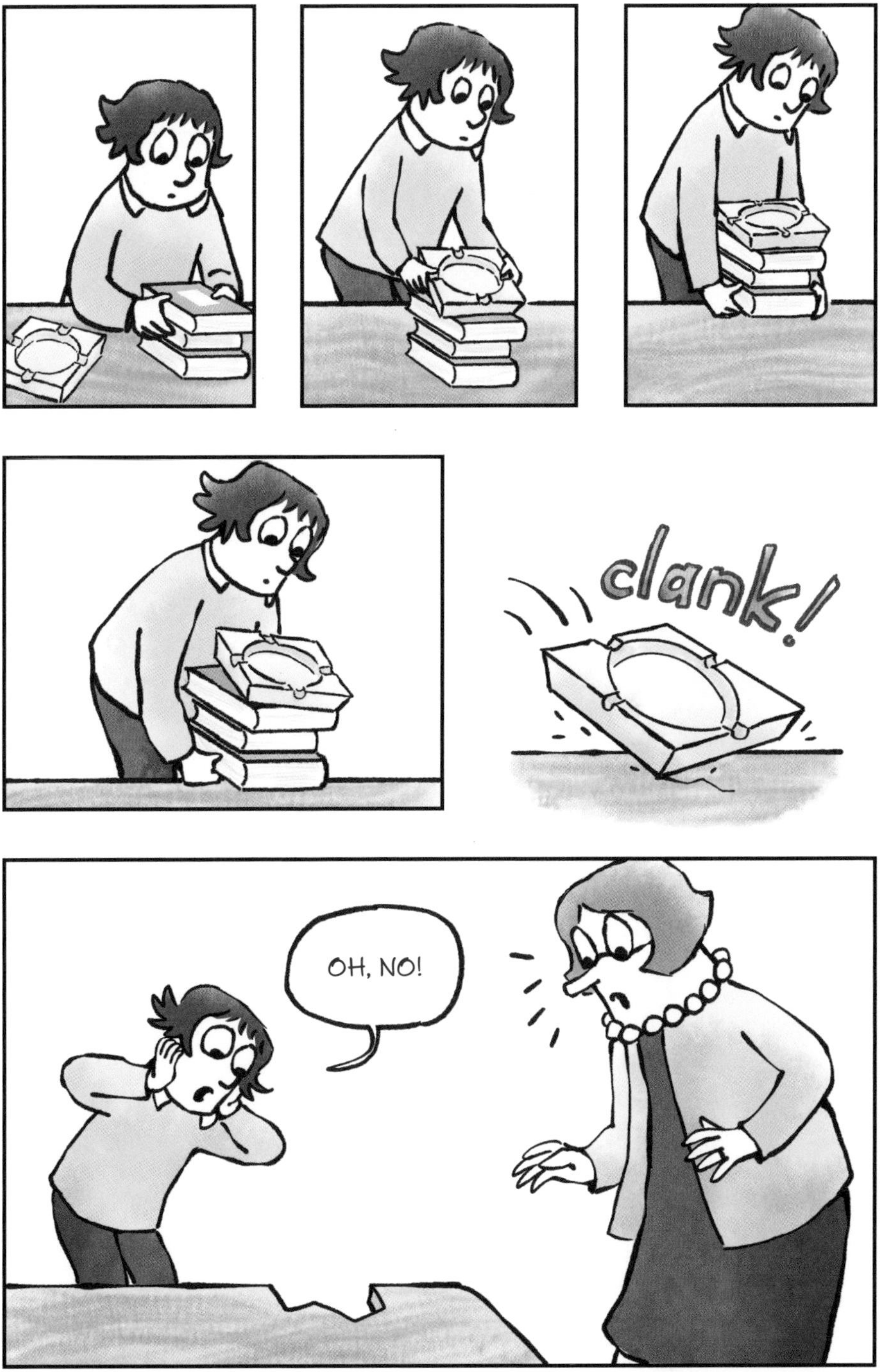
clank!
OH, NO!

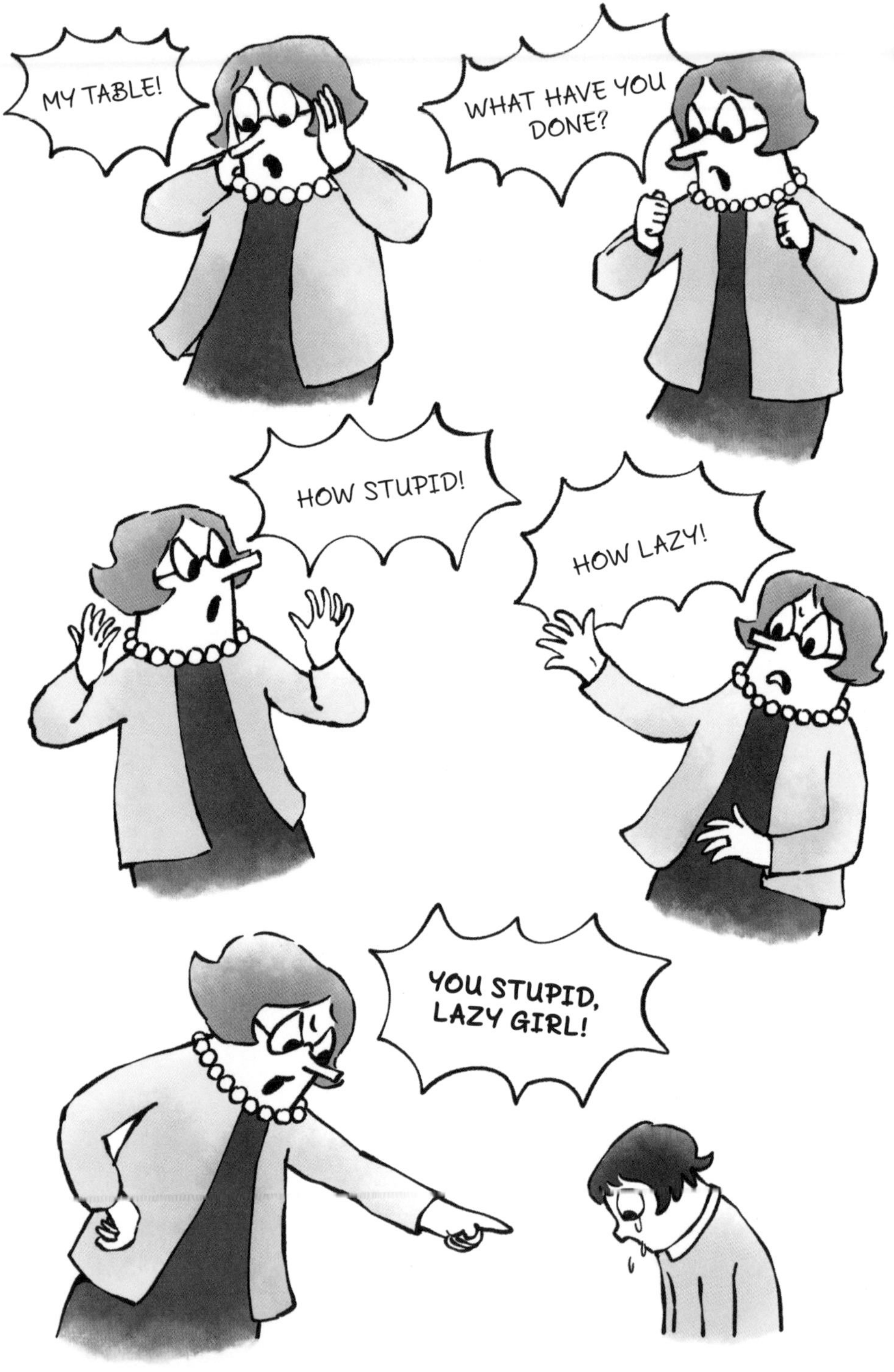
MY TABLE!
WHAT HAVE YOU DONE?
HOW STUPID!
HOW LAZY!
YOU STUPID, LAZY GIRL!

Mom was so angry, she stopped talking to me.
For three days!

Eventually the tabletop was mended.

But I had made up my mind!

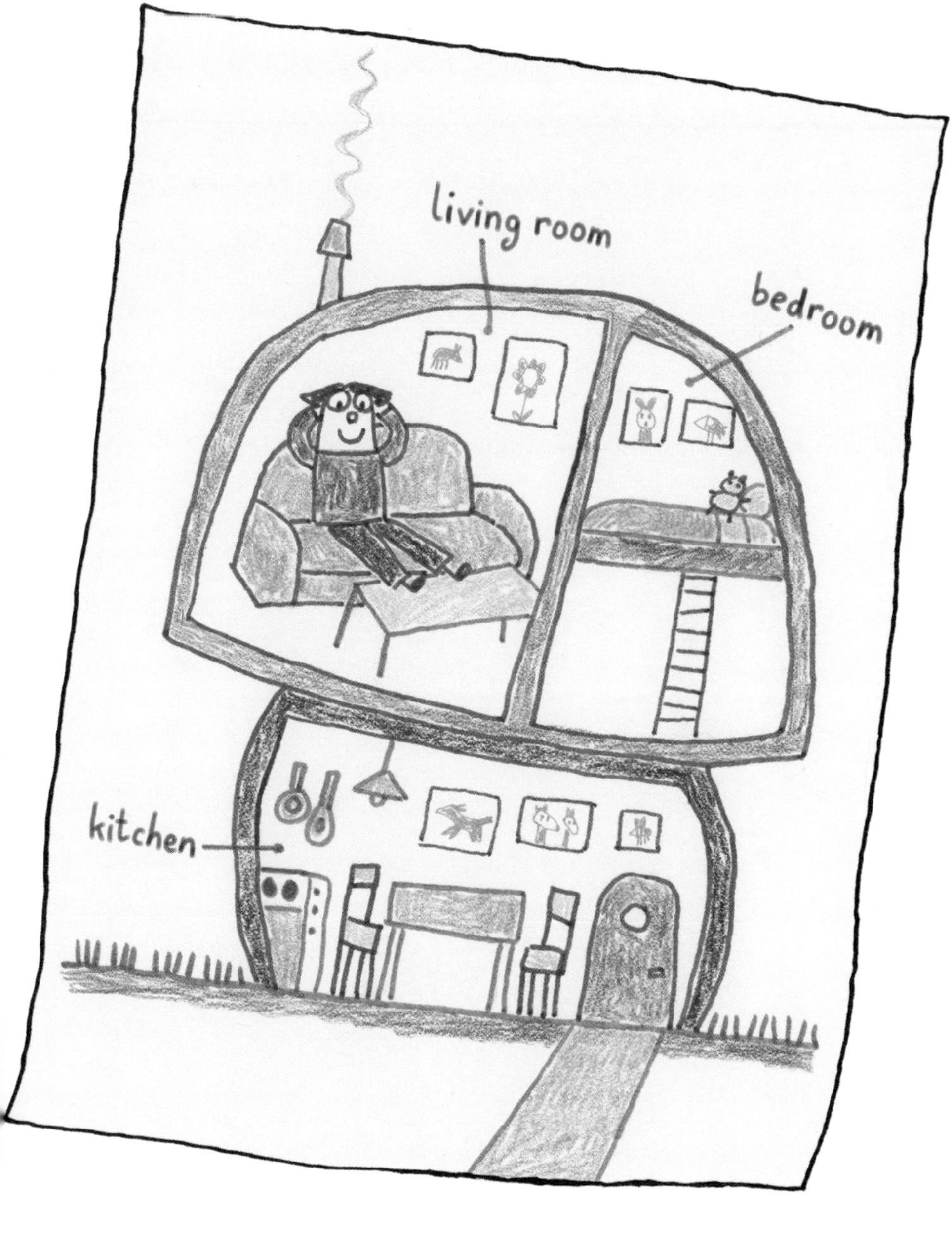
living room
bedroom
kitchen

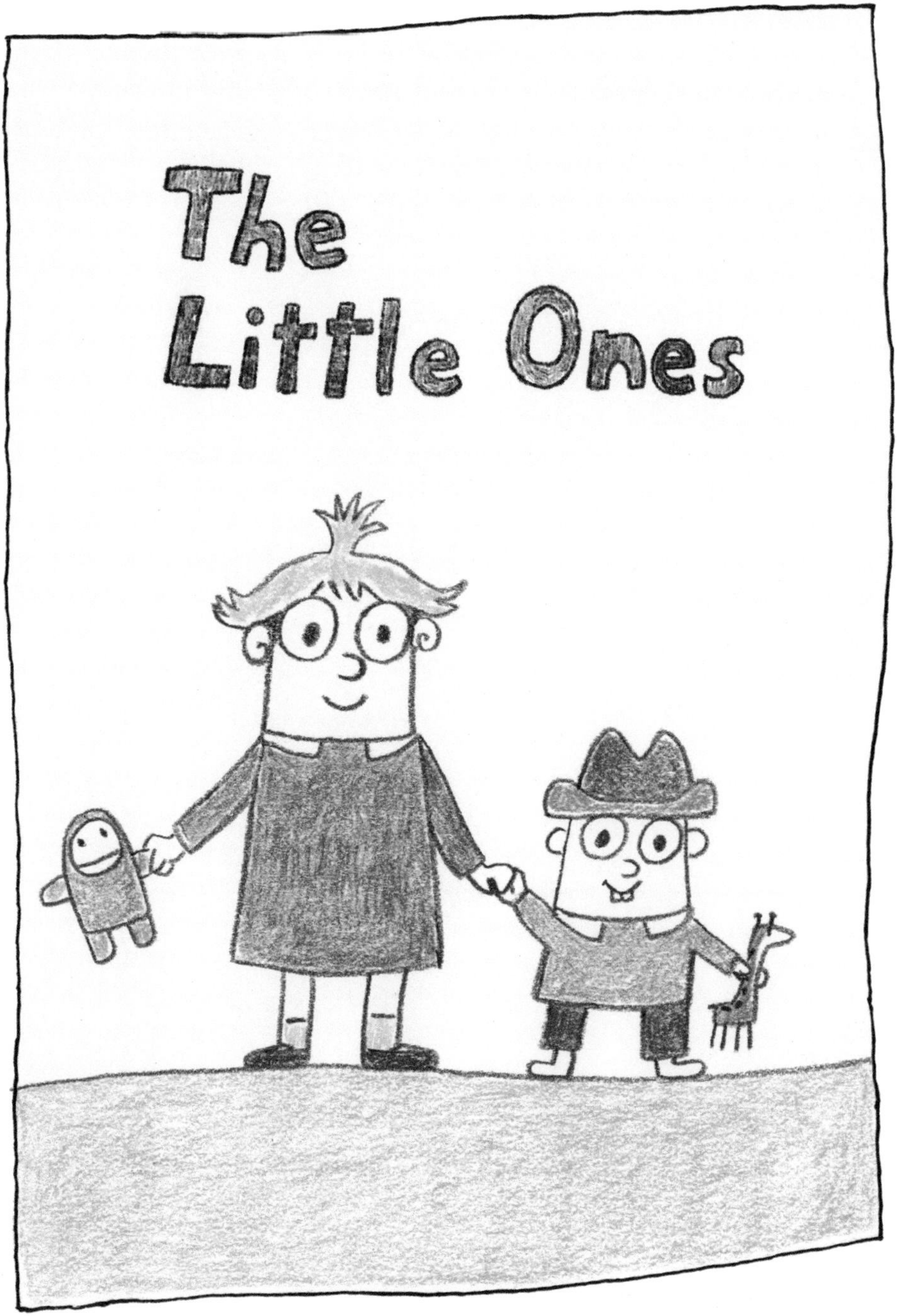
The Little Ones

I was eight when Mom got pregnant. She let us touch her belly, and I felt the baby kicking.

I was so hoping for a girl. And Evita was born!

Dad took Alibert and me to the maternity ward to see her.

At first, Evita was boring.

But soon enough, she was fun to play with.

Evita was so good-natured. Christine and I
readily included her in our games.

I have an idea. Let's dress Evita up.

Your sister is so sweet, Sylvie.

MOM!

Reading to her was safer. And such a good excuse
to enjoy my old picture books again.

Once, Alibert and Evita were
playing on their own.

They climbed all the
way to the garage roof.

The roof gave out, and
Evita fell through.

She was stunned. The doctor was called in.

Make sure she doesn't fall
asleep for a few hours.

That day, our parents were going to a
special event. Something to do with Dad's work.
I was left in charge.

Mom took a lot of pride in Dad's position.
After all, she was the Wife of the Principal!

After Evita's fall, I knew Mom wouldn't want to miss the event. But I was scared!

Alibert felt guilty and made himself scarce.

I was terrified.

What if Evita fell asleep and I couldn't
wake her up? What if she died?

Our parents were gone a long time.

In the end Evita was fine.
But that day, I learned
a new kind of fear.

I was eleven when Mom got pregnant again.

Alibert's wish was granted.

There was something comfortable about the new family composition.

This time, I was fascinated by the new baby.

I took pride in his baby accomplishments.

Just like Alibert and me, Evita and Davido were three years apart.

They were referred to as "the little ones."
Alibert and I became "the big ones."

Unlike Alibert and me, however, the little ones got along famously, right from the start.

Once, I noticed Davido sitting by the bathroom door.

After Davido was born, Mom took some time off from teaching. Still, I was asked to help a lot.

One of my tasks was to hang the laundry to dry in the attic.

I had started reading the adventures of Arsène Lupin and developed a crush on this handsome gentleman burglar.

I turned my laundry chores into thrilling secret meetings with daring Arsène.

When Evita was older, it was my job to walk her
to kindergarten on my way to school.

I learned a new song at school.

Here, Evita. Climb up!

I loved my sister's sweet voice.

Mom did not approve of piggyback rides.

Sylvie, it's not feminine.

Being "feminine" was important to Mom.

Put this on, Sylvie. It's more feminine.

Stop whistling, honey. It's not feminine.

Enough gum, already! Really not feminine!

110

It didn't feel that important to me.

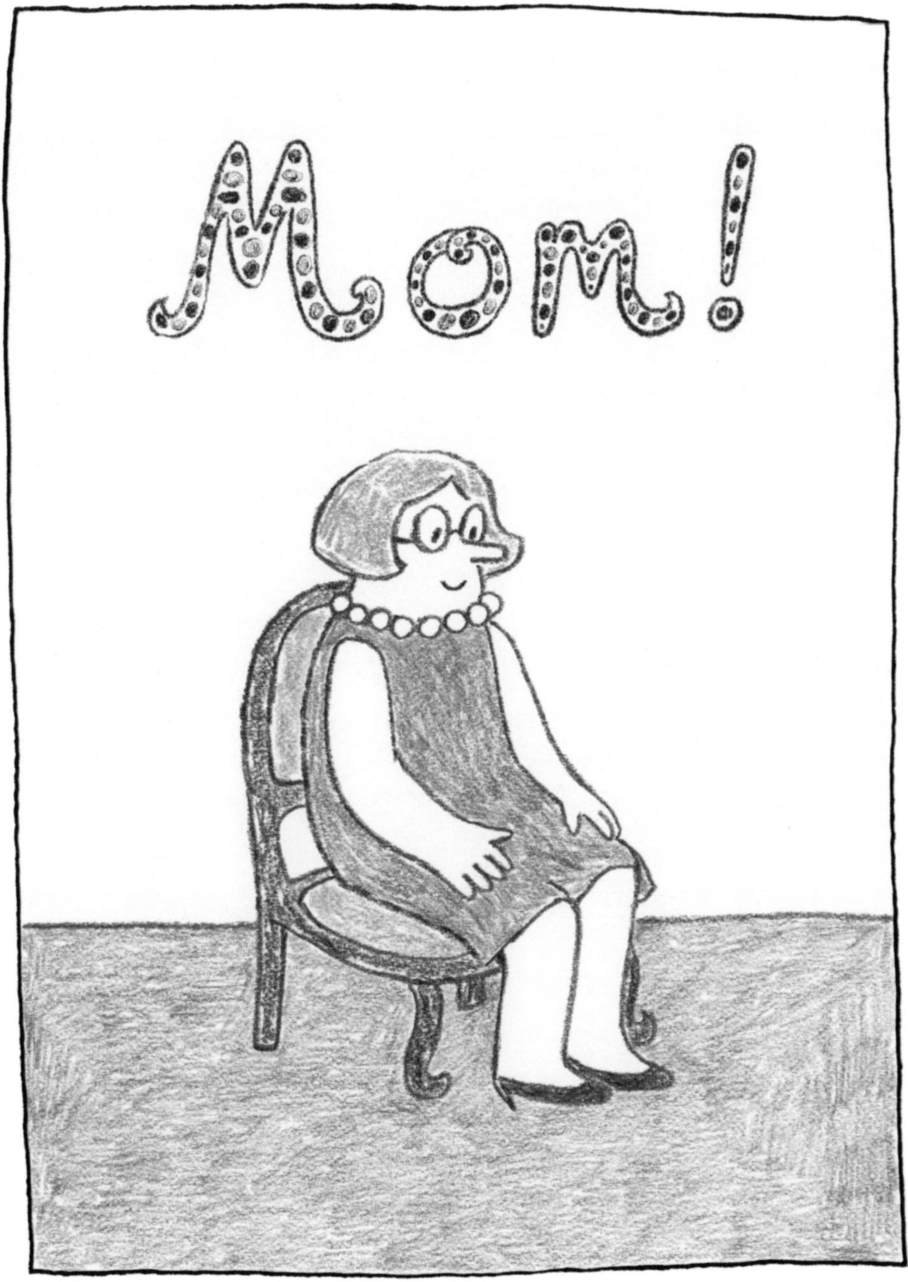
Mom!

Mom always took some figuring out.

When I was little, she was fond of asking:

The trick was to answer:

But to give the impression **she** was the favorite.

It was important to make Mom happy.
Otherwise she was quick to anger.

I became expert at evaluating Mom's mood.

I learned when to agree with her no matter what.

Uh-oh, not the right moment!

And I soaked my shoes, as I was told.

Later . . .

What in the world are you doing to your leather shoes?

But . . . you told me to soak them!

I meant your canvas sneakers, of course!

What a funny misunderstanding!

Haha

Ha ha

Whew!

Mom was obsessed with cleanliness.

The house had to be immaculate at all times.

Alibert had a real knack for driving Mom crazy!

Once, when he was six or seven, he was sent to spend the afternoon with some friends.

Alibert bought the tarts, ate them all, and spent the afternoon roaming through town.

Every day, he made Mom angry for one reason or another.

Sometimes Mom got terrible migraines.

Somehow the migraines seemed to be Alibert's fault.

His struggles at school didn't help.

Poor Alibert!

Eventually, Dad came up with a plan.

After Alibert left, the house became quieter.

Unfortunately, Alibert's absence didn't ease the tension between Mom and Dad.

Dad couldn't do anything right.

Why did you get this brand?

PÂTES*

*Pasta

Wrong turn again?

Your dad! Look how he hung this!

Why is she angry all the time?

Dad isn't so bad.

Once, I asked some questions.

I noticed she hadn't exactly
answered my question.

I hope you make a better match than I did!

A nice boy! From a good family!

You mean a RICH family!

Mom! I don't really care about money!

Oh, it's not the money.

It's your position in life.

Your father needs to keep advancing his career!

But Dad is a PRINCIPAL now!

When your dad was a student in Paris, his professors knew he had unusual potential.

If he applied himself, he could go even further!

But Mom, Dad isn't a bad man!

When we were both young teachers in Morocco, I had high hopes for your dad.

With his writing skills, he could have become a famous writer!

Mom had made up her mind. Whatever Dad did, it would not be enough!

Maybe you should get a divorce?

NEVER!

For the sake of the children!

Mom was fond of dramatic pronouncements!

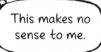

This makes no sense to me.

Mom and Dad sure were different! Once, I went to
a talk my dad was giving on early education.

Wow!
My dad was
fascinating!

Mom, however, had nothing good to say about teaching.

At times, Mom could be so exasperating.

I'm the wife of the principal. Are these your best potatoes?

She always wants special treatment. How embarrassing!

WHAT DID YOU DO?

Poor Alibert! She doesn't need to get that angry!

Sylvie got the best grade in the whole school.

That's not true! Why must she brag so much?

And then there was the Look,
the dreaded Look!

And yet at other times
she could be so attentive!

Was I allowed to feel so conflicted
about my own mother?
Could I feel shame and anger
and still love her?
I didn't know.

I would find refuge from these
troubling thoughts by concentrating on
an elaborate drawing.

During a school break, Alibert came home.

Suddenly he was almost my size, and his voice alternated between squeaks and rumbles.

I'm studying to become an accountant.

I like numbers.

Wow! Alibert knows what he wants to do.

Do you miss home?

No.

Not with Mom always getting mad at me.

She still gets mad at Dad a lot.

Could Alibert be right?
Could someone actually
<u>like</u> being angry?

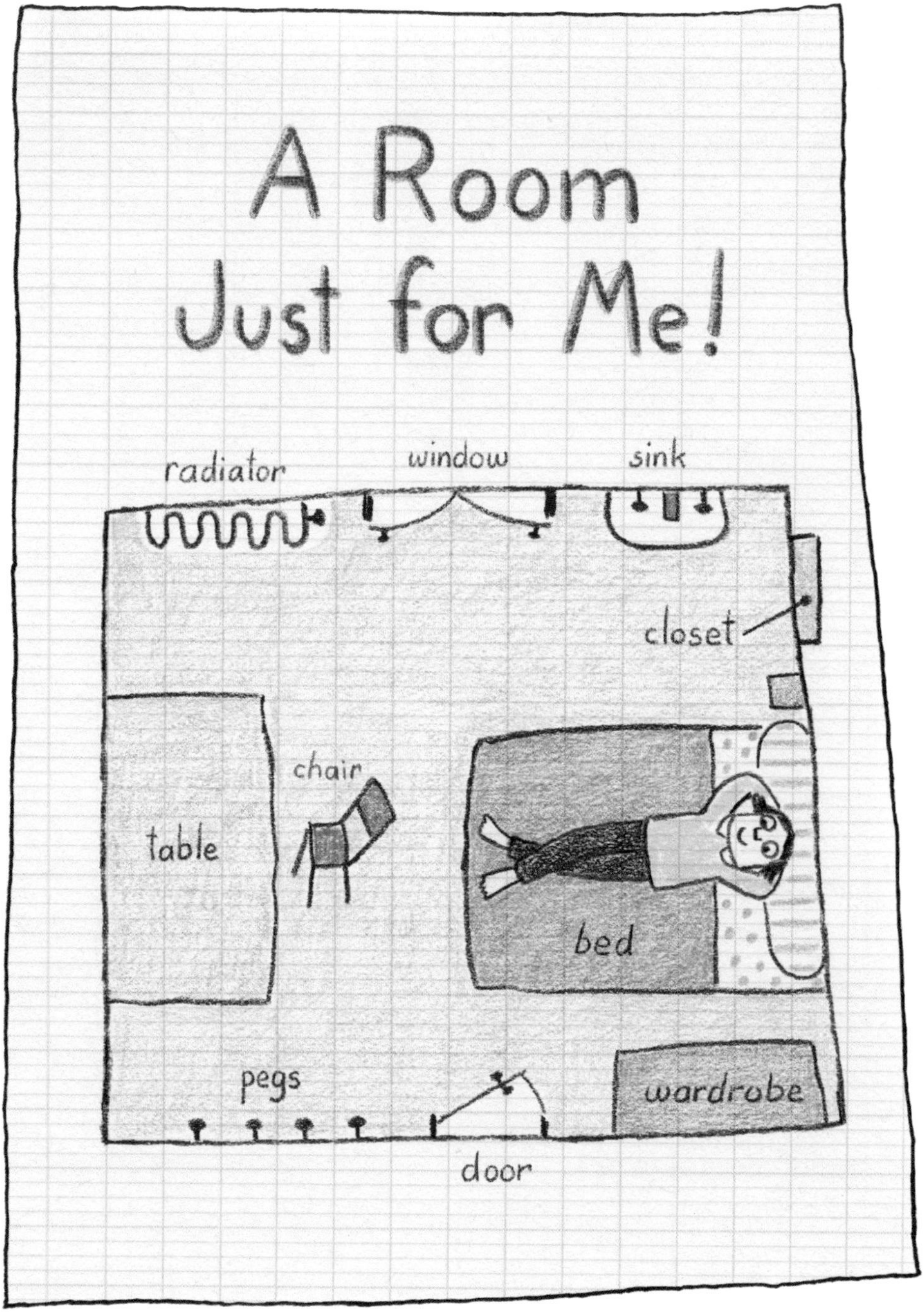
A Room
Just for Me!
radiator
window
sink
closet
chair
table
bed
pegs
wardrobe
door

Out the side door of our apartment,

up the back stairs,

past a bathroom,

past the apartment of a janitor,

there was a small empty room.

I dreamed of making it my room.
But I knew I would need to be convincing.

And Mom agreed!

I spent hours cleaning and organizing
my new space.

I remembered this phrase from school:

UNE PLACE POUR CHAQUE CHOSE ET
CHAQUE CHOSE À SA PLACE.

A SPOT FOR EACH ITEM
AND EACH ITEM IN ITS SPOT.

These words gave me
a wonderful sense
of peace and security.

shelf

desk

closet

sink shelf

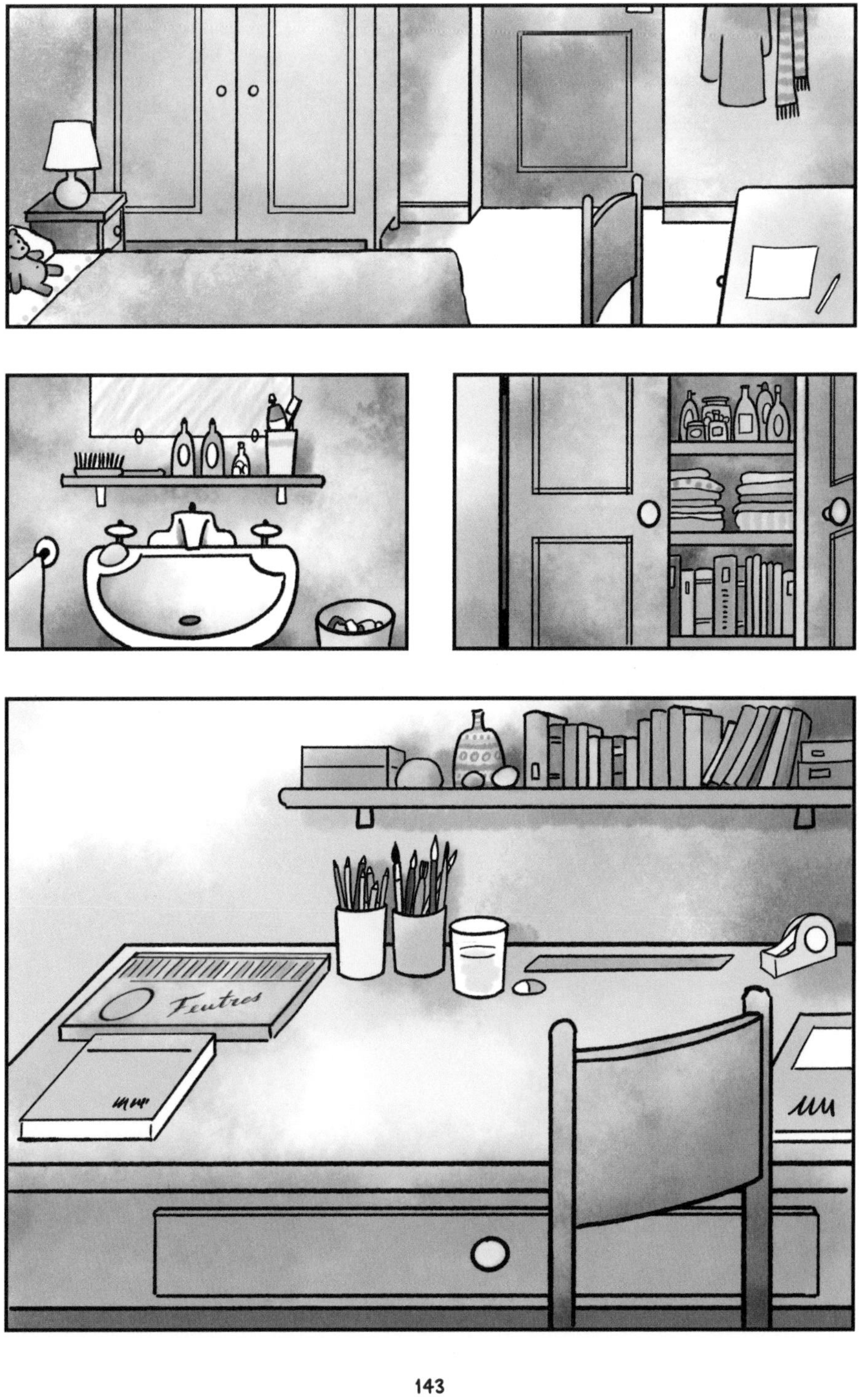
Feutres

The furniture was shabby, the linoleum
floor lumpy. But I had my very own key to
my very own kingdom . . .

far from the family noises, far from the tension between my parents.

The window overlooked
the courtyard of the
nursing home next door.
It was always very quiet
out there.

I often saw an old couple sitting
quietly on a bench in the sun.
They seemed content just to sit together.

It was now up to me to wake up on
time every morning.

I fell for the "earmuffs."

The alarm clock did the trick, all right.

But it also kept me up at night.

I ended up burying it under my sweaters every night before going to sleep.

The good thing was I **had** to get out of bed to silence it.

The room was my private domain. The little ones were the only ones I ever brought up there.

It was where I could be in my own world of books, drawings, and romantic dreams.

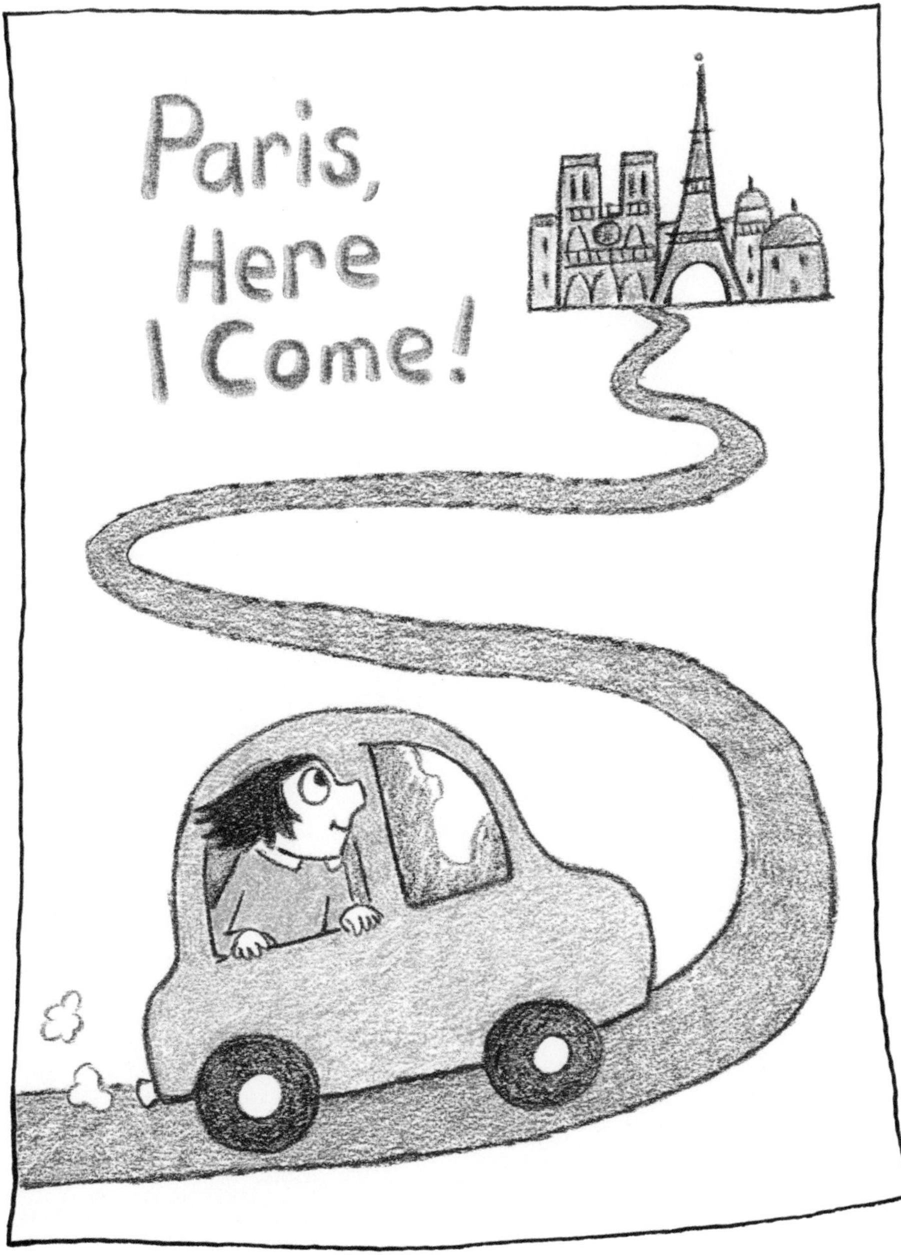
Paris,
Here
I Come!

My fifteenth birthday was approaching.

I had **loved** that trip! And now Dad was talking about going again! But just me this time! **Wow!**

We ate in cafés.

It was so nice having Dad to myself for a change!

One day, we went to the Luxembourg Gardens.

Before entering the garden,
Dad bought a baguette.

There were so many beautiful statues.
I was mesmerized.

I had a feeling you would like these, Sylvette.

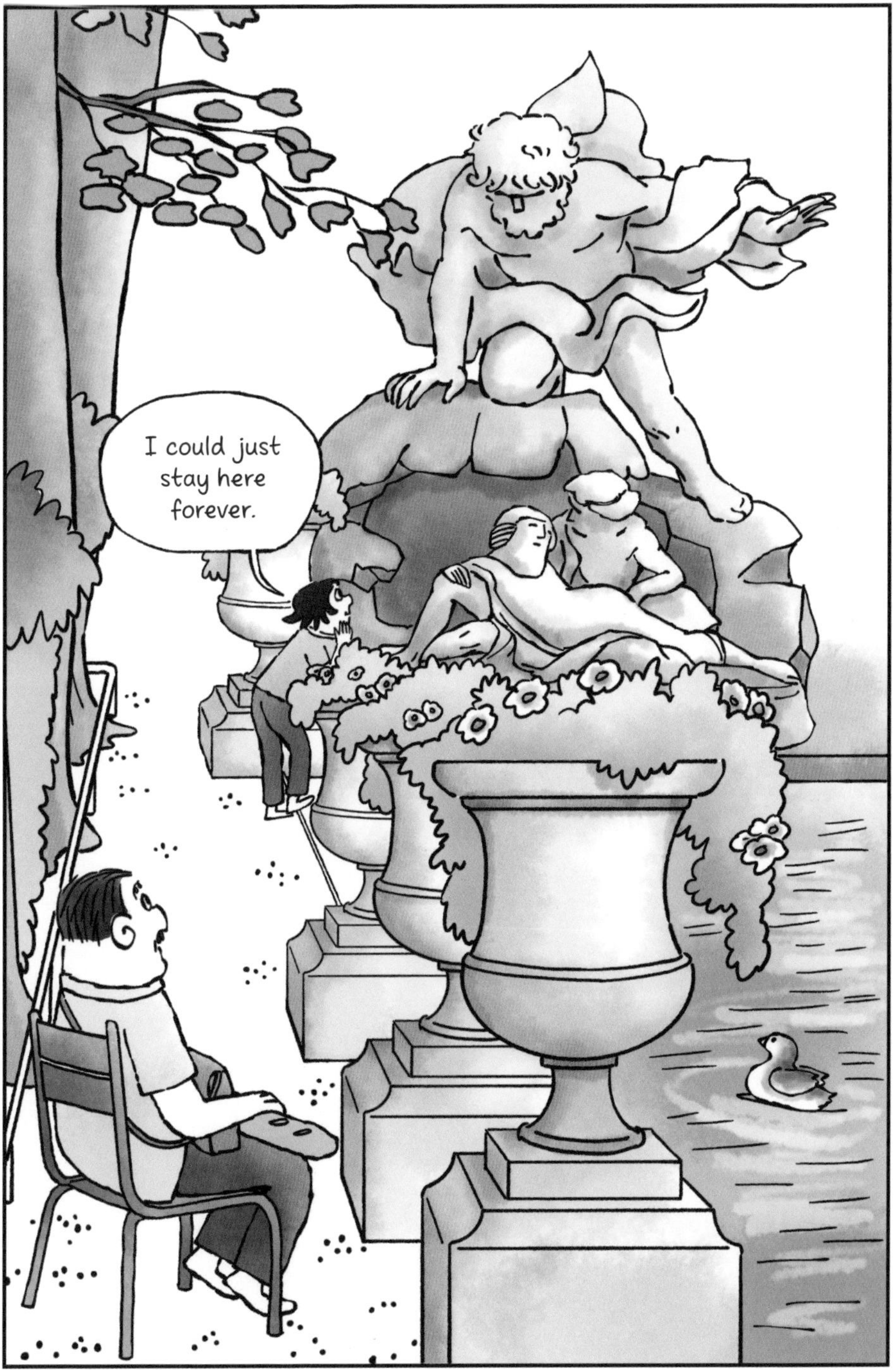
I could just stay here forever.

But Dad, what about the baguette?

Ha ha! Let's find the sparrows.

Yes, this is a perfect spot.

Now, fill your hand with crumbs.

And sit very still with your hand out.

It took a long time, but it was well worth it.

Another day, we went to the Place du Tertre.

First there was a lot of stair-climbing.

And suddenly, at the top, it was like an open-air artist work space.

Of all the displayed art, one set really caught my fancy.

Dad, look at these.

Dad let me choose one of the drawings.
For my room!

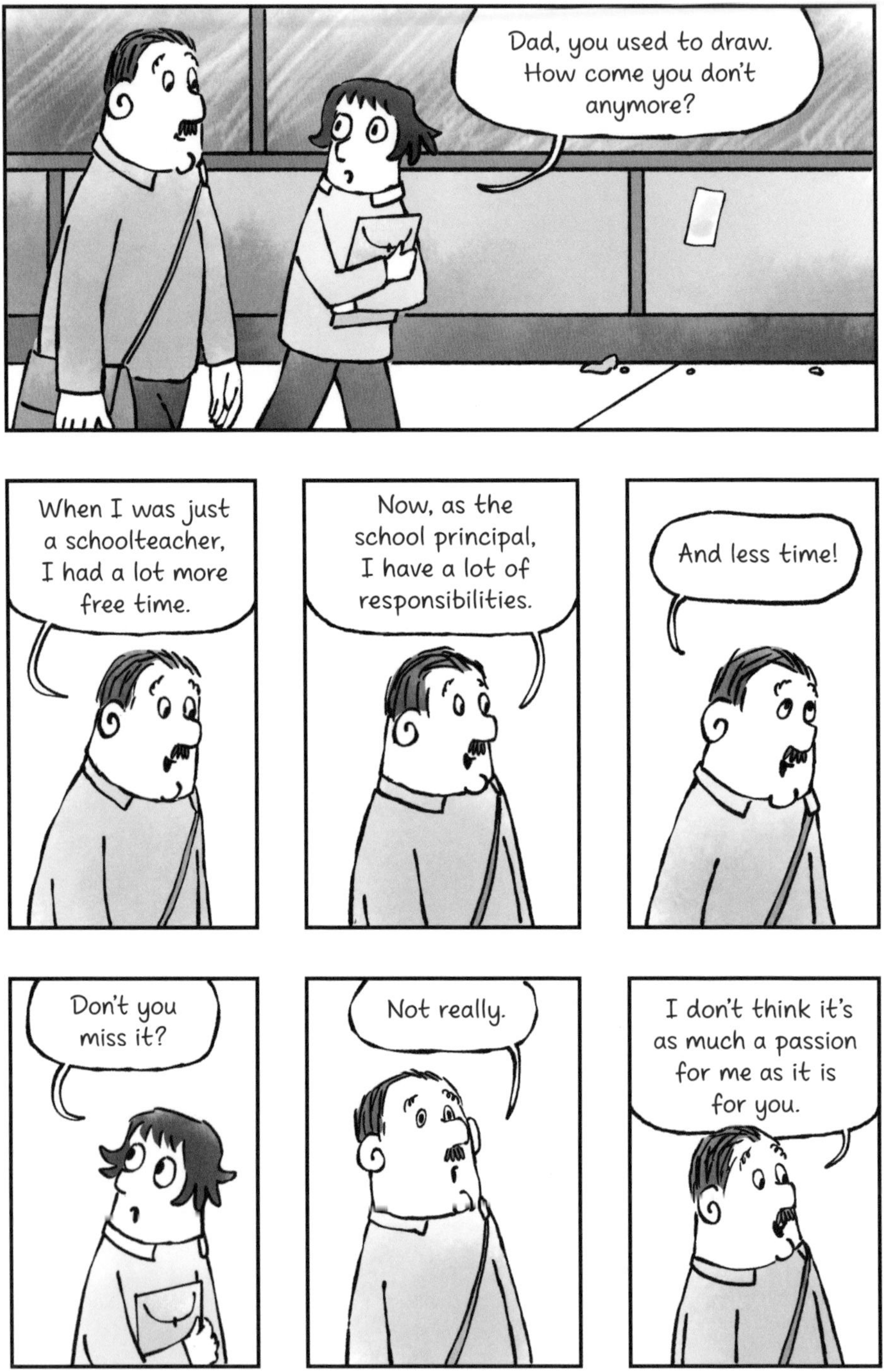
Dad, you used to draw. How come you don't anymore?
When I was just a schoolteacher, I had a lot more free time.
Now, as the school principal, I have a lot of responsibilities.
And less time!
Don't you miss it?
Not really.
I don't think it's as much a passion for me as it is for you.

But Dad . . .

Do you like your work?

I do, Sylvette. I really do!

Training good teachers feels very important to me!

Sometimes when I see you with Evita and Davido, I think you would make a terrific teacher!

Really? Me?

Too Much Homework!
Help!
Math
Essay
French
Biology
Physics
Spelling
Essay
English
Literature
Geography
History
Math
Grammar

Elementary school had been easy. Fun, even!

In middle school, it started to get hard.

By ninth grade, I was really struggling.

So much seemed to depend on the
dreaded report card.

Of course, this didn't apply to elective classes.

I worked hard and thankfully managed to get decent grades.

Of course, that meant free time depended entirely on homework.

There was never enough time for my own reading and drawing.

Occasionally, I would seek parental help.

Mom, I'm completely stuck.

Go and ask Dad for help.

My dad must have loved homework. His way of helping was to do the whole thing himself.

. . . and the fish rolled its globulous eyes toward me. . . .

I changed a few words here and there, but I never felt good about these assignments.

Very good work, Sylvie.

Gulp

Mom was helpful too. Especially with memorization.

She also taught me many practical things:

Sewing.

Baking.

And, one day, how to fix an electric switch.

She even taught me to knit. I never went beyond the obvious scarf motif, though.

Mom, I can't figure out how to stop this thing!

Occasionally, there was one advantage
to homework.

I still have to finish my essay and study for my math test.

Skip the dishes tonight, honey, and go straight to work.

Mostly, though, I felt caught in a cycle of
homework and chores.

Yay! I'm all done with homework! I have time to read and draw!

That's good, honey. But first you need to vacuum, iron the shirts, and scrub the tub.

Sigh

In eighth grade, Christine and I started to study together. Homework didn't feel quite so painful that way.

Christine lived with her mother, her grandmother, an older sister, and a very old dog.

Their little world of women seemed so peaceful to me.

Christine's mother was the school nurse, and they had a small apartment just by the infirmary, in the dorm building of the school.

We did our homework at the dining room table, munching endlessly on cookies and chocolate.

Christine never talked about her father.
There was a framed picture of a man in uniform
on the sideboard.

One night I stayed for a sleepover.
Her bedroom was too tiny for two, so we slept
in the infirmary next door.

I'm so sorry, Christine!

It's all right, mostly.

What bugs me sometimes is how all the others have a dad and I don't.

I hate being different!

Her too?

But really, we are ALL different!

In one way or another.

And some differences come from US!

Like how you love science.

And how you love to draw!

177

One spring, we got into the habit of playing
Ping-Pong in the school break room.

We were very pleased with our Ping-Pong skills:
we could keep the ball going back and forth . . .
back and forth . . . endlessly.

Once, a friend of Christine's sister joined us. She belonged to a Ping-Pong club.

We found out what "real" Ping-Pong was like.

We *didn't* play as much after that.

Our first year of high school,
Christine was not as available as usual.

Want to get
together
tomorrow?

OK.
Thursday,
then?

How about
next week?

That summer, I saw her at the swimming pool,
playing the "square" game: two boys and two girls
lying in a square.

It seemed like the most boring game to me.

And then I noticed a boy gazing at her with a goofy look on his face.

Romance was also on my mind. But I found no appeal in the boys from school.

How could they ever compare with my book heroes?

That was the summer Christine and her family
moved to Lyon.

After she moved, we talked on the phone
a few times.

*It was easier to be friends
when we saw each other
almost every day.*

On one hand, I was missing her.

On the other hand, we had started to drift apart.

I needed to make new friends.

My friends were impressed with
my home in a school.

We hung out in the auditorium . . .

or outside in the bushes, sharing secret dreams.

One day, my being Jewish was mentioned. . . .

You're Jewish?

Oh, I love Jewish people!

That's an odd thing to say!

How could one love all people of any particular group?

I get it! She wants me to feel comfortable!

Personally, I believe all people should be treated as equals!

WOW!

We didn't talk more about it. But it felt good to hear kind words coming from my friends.

I Love
DRAWING
More than
ANYTHING

In our hallway were four pictures Dad had painted when he was young. As far back as I can remember, they filled me with admiration.

I also loved looking at our collection of art books.

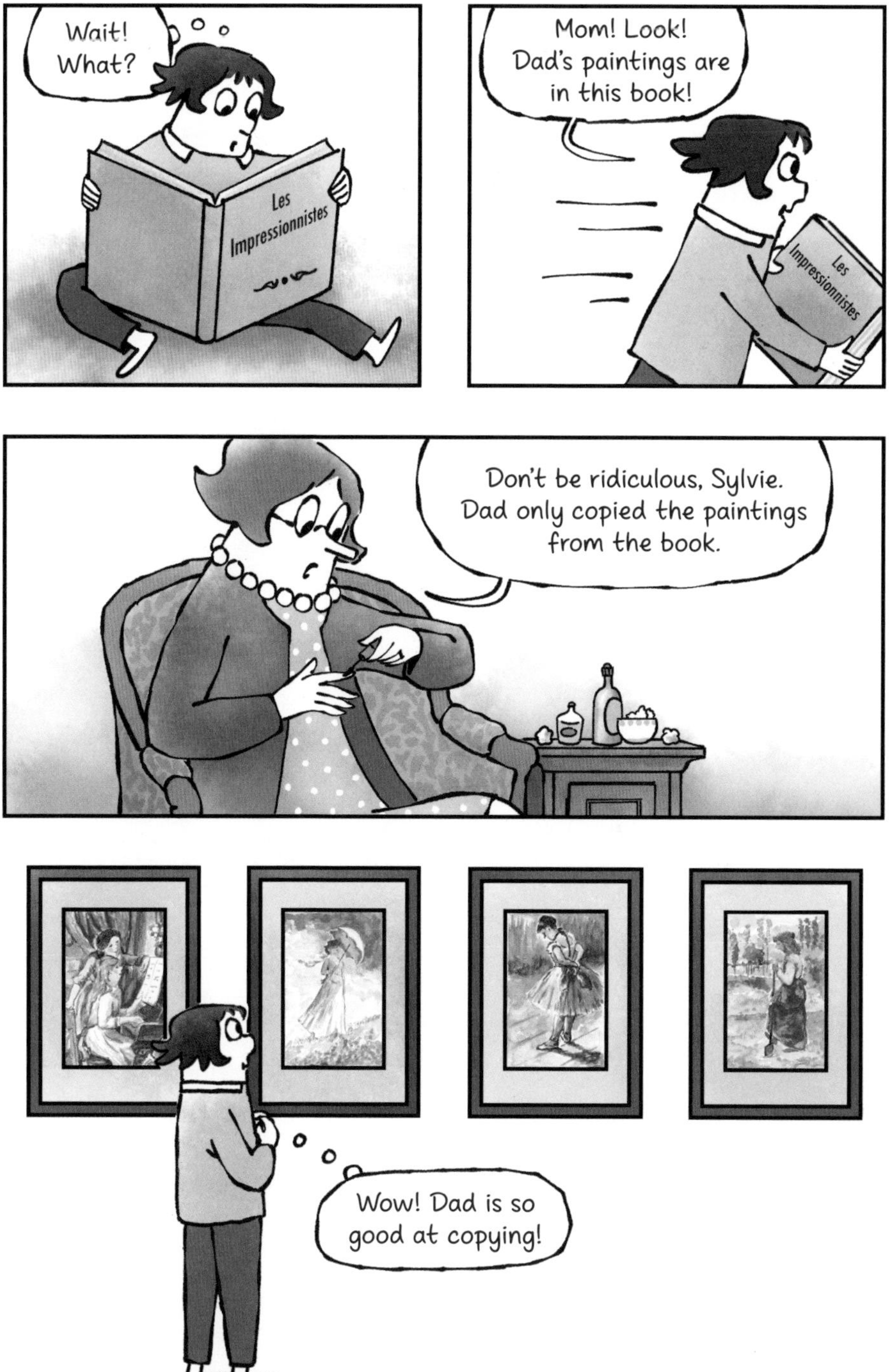
Wait! What?
Les Impressionnistes
Mom! Look! Dad's paintings are in this book!
Les Impressionnistes
Don't be ridiculous, Sylvie. Dad only copied the paintings from the book.
Wow! Dad is so good at copying!

I never saw Dad paint, but when we were little,
we could always get him to draw for us.

I was so proud, I once took
one of his drawings to school.

Now it was my turn to amuse Evita and Davido with my drawings.

They usually ended up busy with their own drawings.

I was proud of them and their ideas.

My own favorite was to draw from comic books.

But I also drew from imagination, art books, and magazines.

I was in awe of my own power.
One moment the page was blank.
A bit later, it contained a whole world.

There was no question in my mind
that drawing was what I liked
to do more than ANYTHING!

Mom didn't draw. Embroidery was her thing.
But she seemed to enjoy my drawings.

Very nice, honey.

However, I really wished she wouldn't show them off to all visitors.

Sylvie, bring your latest drawing to show Madame Vuillard.

Lovely!

If only she spent as much time on her homework.

What a weird thing for Mom to say!
We all knew that Dad was the one who could draw.
Then she added:

Could Mom be serious?
She looked serious!

For years, my parents let me take
an art class downtown, once a week, with
Monsieur Carthélémy.

He had so many different ideas.

As the years went by, the assignments became more elaborate.

A copy of a tapestry.

A study of our hands.

A scary dream.

An antipollution poster.

But no matter the subject,
I loved, loved, loved it all!

At some point, however, I felt I was outgrowing Monsieur Carthélémy's class.

That class is for little kids, really!

I'll just draw on my own.

I was getting more and more critical of my drawings.

This is terrible!

I really can't draw!

scrunch

I need some kind of direction.

Luckily, an art club had just started at school.

New New
ART CLUB
Tuesdays
5:00 - 6:30
Get ready for your art test.

Wow! This is JUST what I need!

Right away, it felt exciting. Monsieur Delorme had dismantled a little book of ink drawings.

Monsieur Delorme let me borrow the loose pages.

In my little attic room, I set out to copy as many as possible.

I became obsessed with ink, with the incredible variety of effects one could achieve with this simplest of materials.

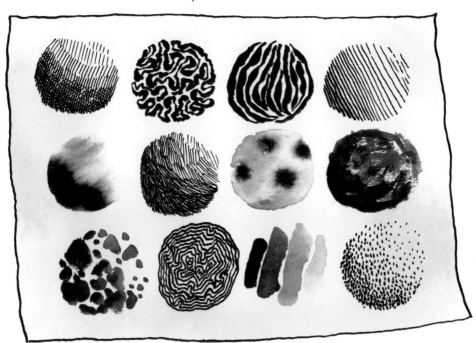

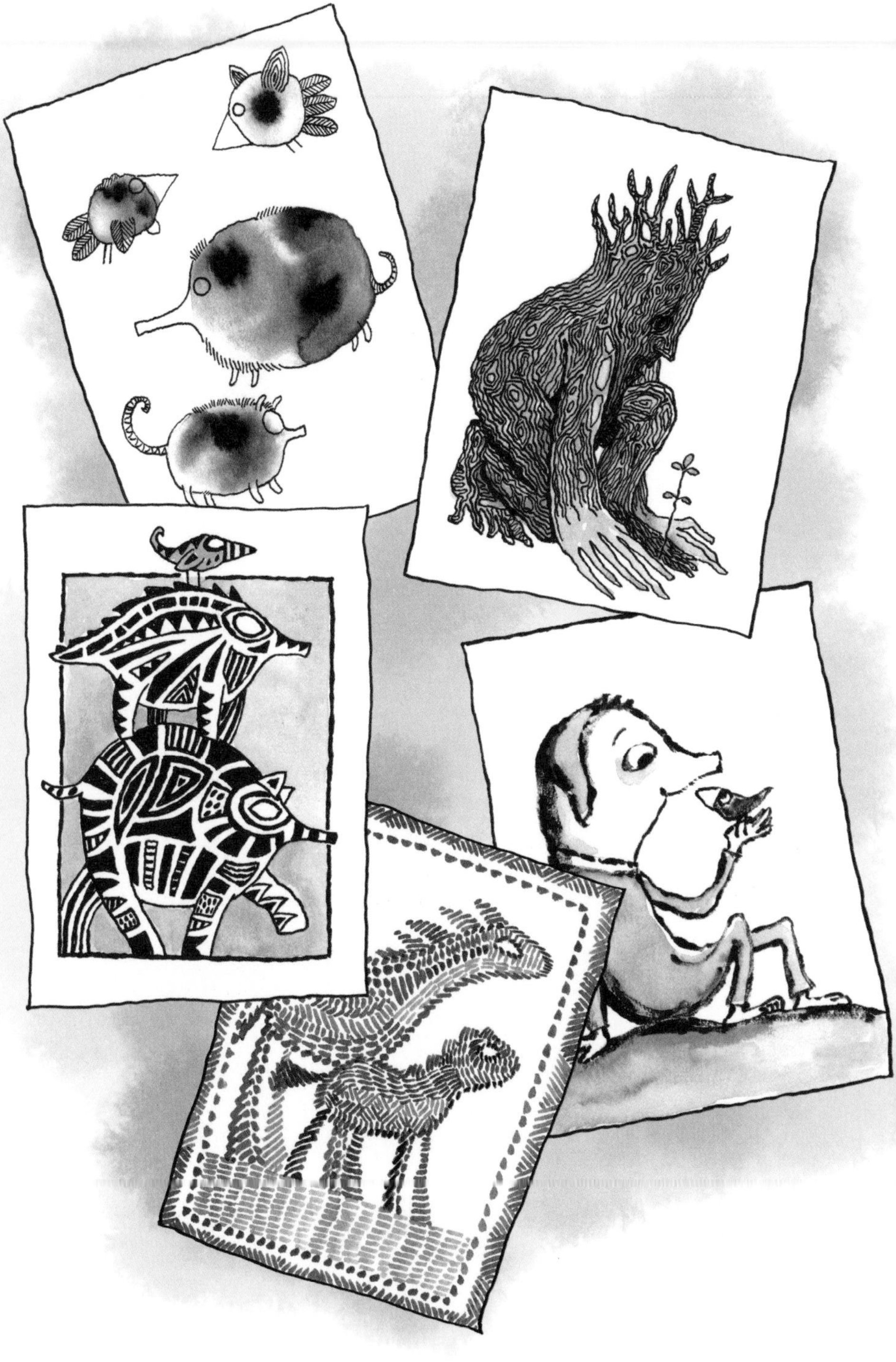

In Monsieur Carthélémy's class, we had mostly used our imagination. With Monsieur Delorme, we were learning practical skills.

We drew one another.

We drew modern still lifes.

We experimented with watercolor.

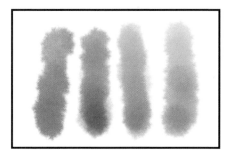

I realized how little I knew.
I felt like a sponge, ready to absorb it all.

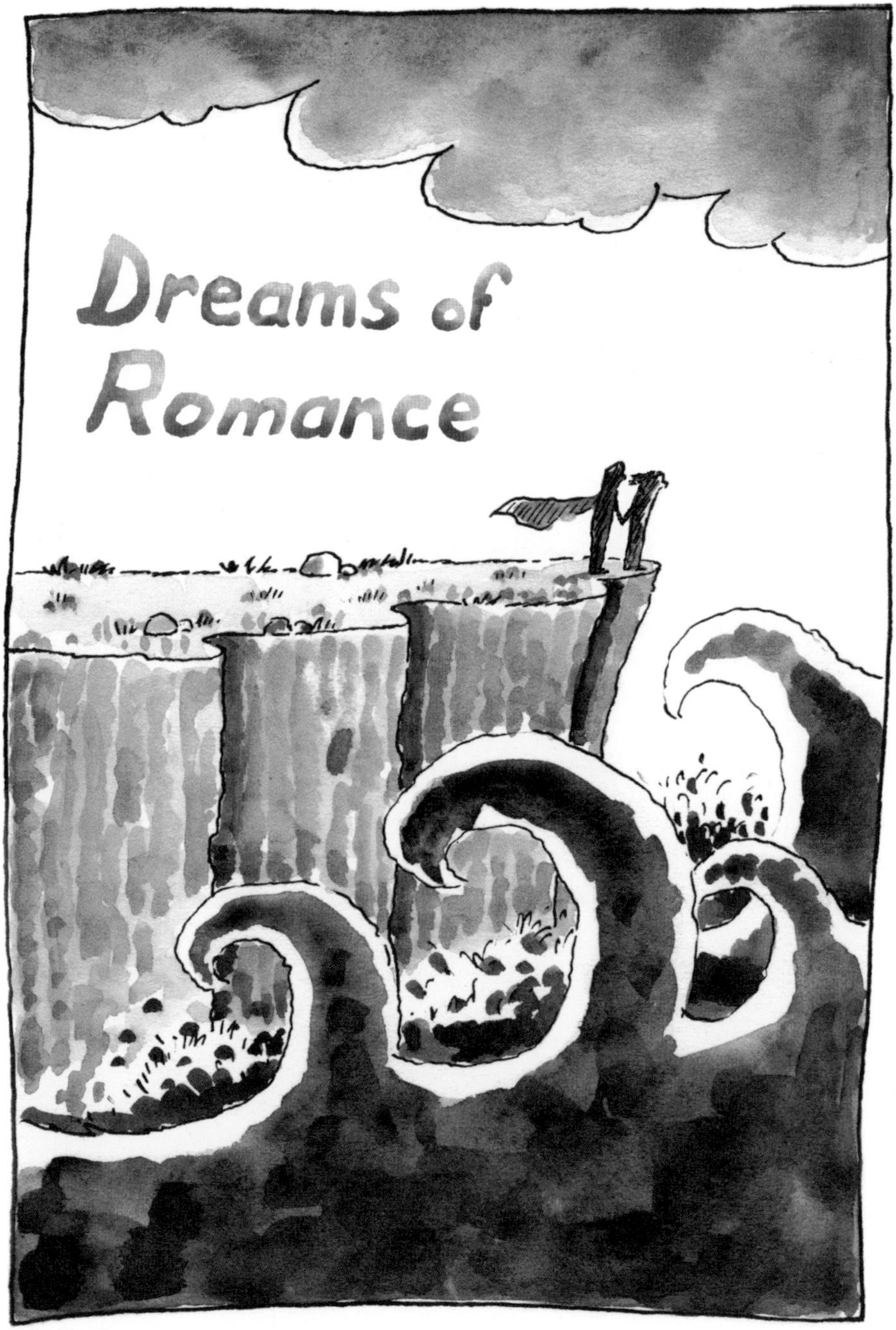
Dreams of Romance

Every summer, we took a long vacation by the shore. Until Davido came along, we had slept in a large family tent.

Now, with four children, we upgraded to a brand-new camper. Alibert, back from school, kept asking to ride in the camper instead of the car. I would have happily shared the space with him.

We were delighted, however, to each get our very own tiny tent. That was even better than sharing the camper!

I organized my little tent, and it became
my private room away from home.

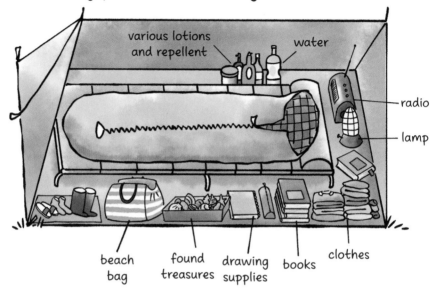

various lotions
and repellent

water

radio

lamp

beach
bag

found
treasures

drawing
supplies

books

clothes

On rainy days, I could spend hours there,
reading, drawing, and listening to popular songs
on my little radio.

I was sixteen when we first discovered Brittany.
I developed a special fondness for its wild
coastline and often drizzly weather.

Bretagne 1976

I had been devouring *Jane Eyre*. The story transported me to a world where a profound love developed against a backdrop of cold and deserted moors. Brittany felt just like that. Romantic encounters were bound to happen here!

A British family was set up next to our spot.
The boy seemed nice. Could romance happen
to me soon?

I hoped my school English was enough
to communicate.

It felt nice, talking with a boy.

Just as well he was leaving.
I didn't want to see this
kid ever again!

Some days, the beach felt too hot,
and I looked for shadier spots.

One day, I took a stroll through the woods.

I indulged in some delicious daydreaming.

Oh, no! I had wandered off the path and arrived at a field surrounded by thorns and brambles.

Behind me, the path had completely vanished.

The cows looked enormous, but I needed to get to the other side of the field.

No choice but to brave the monsters!

Really! Where were my heroes hiding all this time?

Surprisingly, the end of summer felt bittersweet.

Mixed with the sadness of leaving summer behind
was a vague feeling of anticipation.

September meant a new grade, new teachers,
a general sense of starting fresh.

Also new notebooks.
I loved new notebooks.

There was also
the joy of the new
outfit.

And, best of all, school meant seeing my friends again.

*Hi, girls.

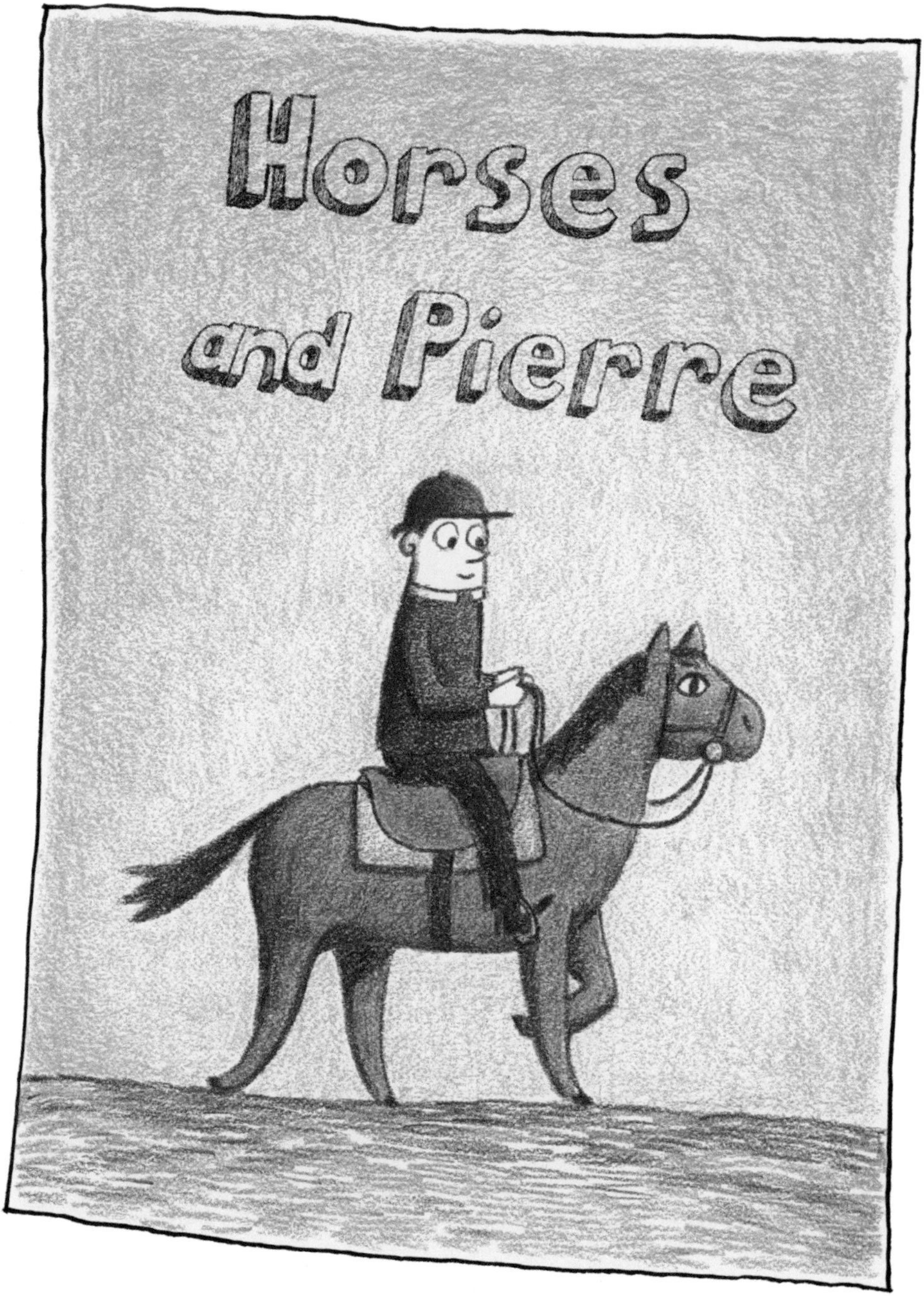
Horses
and Pierre

Gym wasn't really my thing. True, I could run and jump decently. Even rope-climbing wasn't too bad.

That's your best time, Sylvie.

OK. Come down. Your turn, Isabelle.

Good! Keep going!

But the minute a ball was involved, it was disastrous!

Pass! Here! Pass!

I just hope no one throws ME the ball. . . .

My one moment of glory was short-lived.

It was the wrong basket!

And then, in my last year of high school,
I had some luck.

This year, you will have the option to sign up for riding lessons.

Learning to ride would be so cool.

Hey, Brigitte! I'm definitely going!

Me too!

That's where I've been riding for years.

I'm joining the handball team.

Me too.

Swimming for me.

You'll just have to wear comfortable clothes and sturdy shoes. They will have helmets there.

Boys and girls will go together.

For the whole year, every Friday,
a bus took us to the riding stable.

For Brigitte, it was like a second home. But for the rest of us, it was a new world to conquer.

Riding was hard. But there were no grades,
no homework. School seemed so far away.

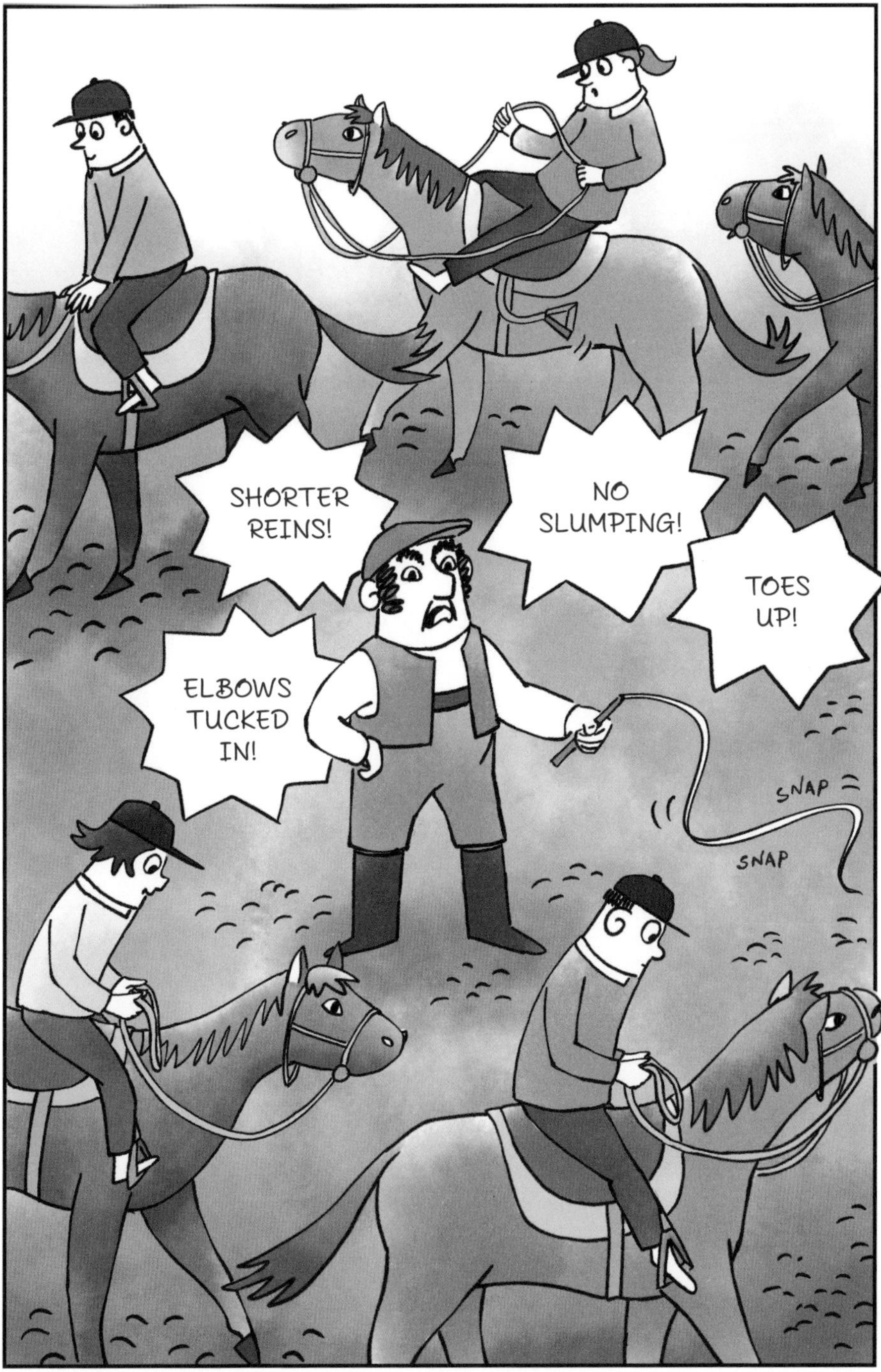

SHORTER REINS!
NO SLUMPING!
TOES UP!
ELBOWS TUCKED IN!
SNAP
SNAP

The barn was freezing. The helmets were musty.

The master was tough. The horses ornery.

The horses must have known they were dealing with beginners.

COME ON! GET BACK ON!

Only Brigitte seemed perfectly at ease and in total control of her horse.

And yet we loved it.
To be riding these
enormous creatures,
it was exhilarating!

It was at these riding
lessons that Brigitte
and I befriended
Pierre, a new student.

The three of us became good friends.

We could be so giggly together, laughing hysterically
for the silliest reason.

It turned out Pierre lived close to my home. He started waiting for me at the street corner.

It was so nice walking to school with him.

I became so eager to see him.

Pierre was now constantly in my thoughts.

But I felt very private about it.

Yet the new feeling was so overwhelming,
I had to tell someone.

Mom, I really
like Pierre
a lot.

Would you like to
invite him over for
lunch on Sunday?

Wow! Mom was so
nice about it.

I'll ask him.

Mom made her delicious gratin dauphinois.

Pierre, would you
like some more?

Soon I was invited to his home.

Oh, no! Was Pierre's mom going to talk about Easter celebration? Church, Mass, and all that?

And the conversation went on without mention of religion or holiday celebration. Whew!

After lunch, we took care of Pierre's little sister.

We listened to his records.

Pierre walked me home. I felt I could tell him anything. I talked about the trouble with my parents.

And he told me about his family.

So his home was also troubled.

I wondered if every family had an ongoing drama, hidden from the outside world.

The days were getting warmer, making it hard
to stay home and study.

Let's finish our homework early and do something on Sunday.

Yeah!

Hey, Pierre! Hey, Sylvie!

Hi, Isabelle!

Isabelle was the girl every boy had a crush on.

Are you guys doing anything on Sunday?

I'm taking care of my little sister.

Oh? Oh, well. Ciao!

wink!

WOW!

Sunday was a beautiful day. We decided to ride our bikes into the countryside.

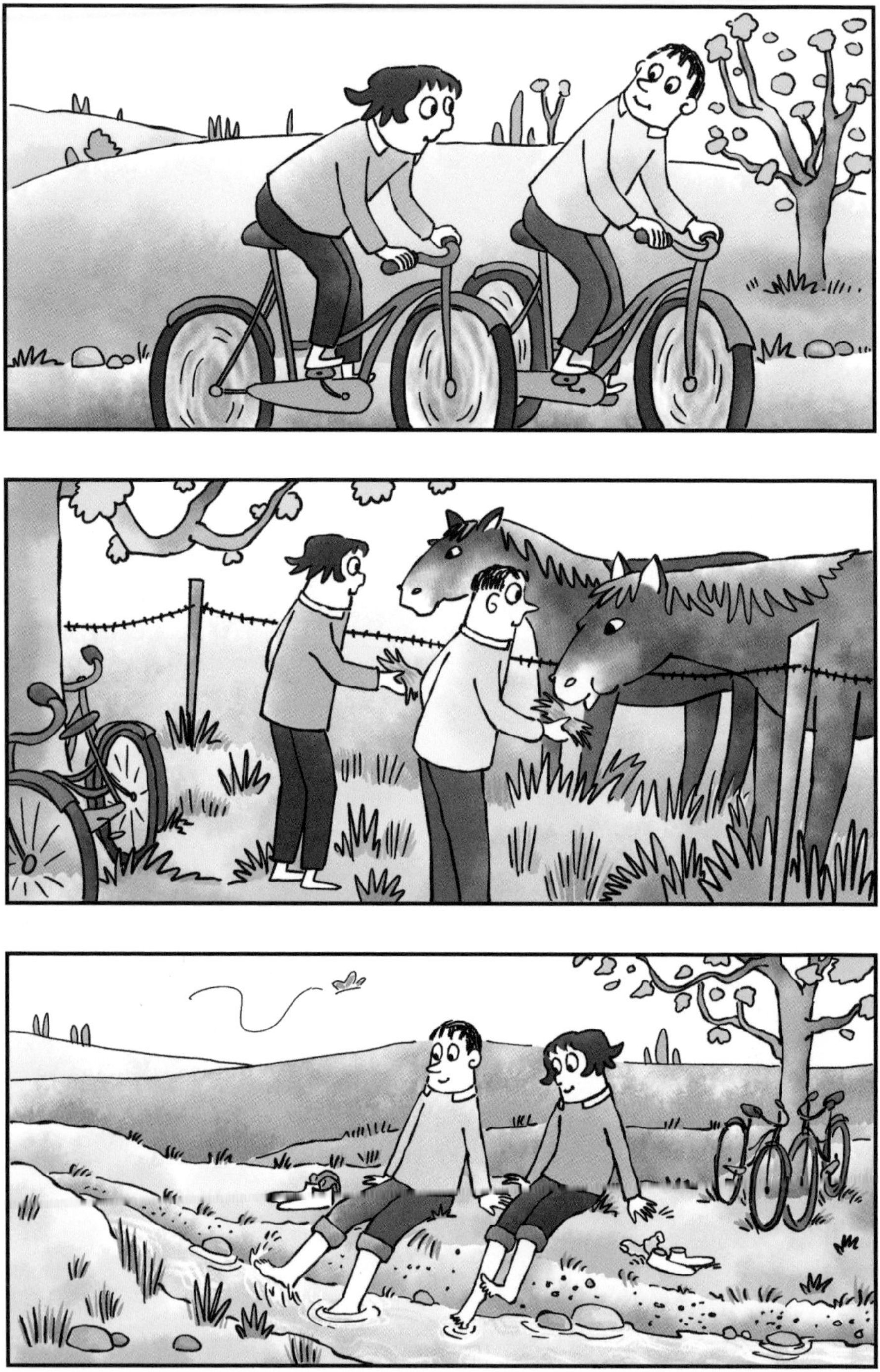

I'm getting hungry.

Look! Let's get some cheese here.

*Goat cheese

I'll get you some cheese.

And I have a fresh loaf of bread.

That's five francs for the cheese and three for the bread.

I'll get you some cider from the cellar.

243

It was the best meal ever!

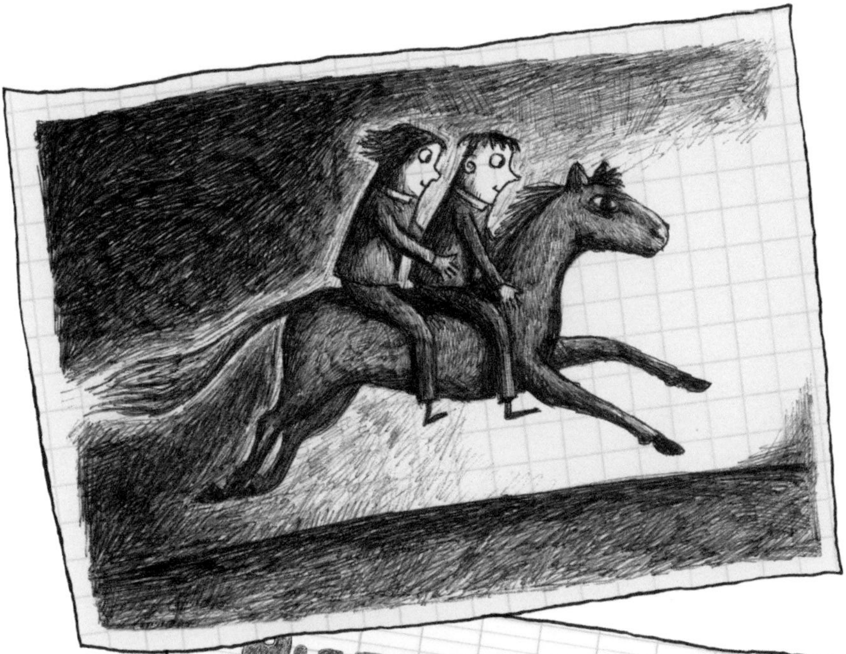

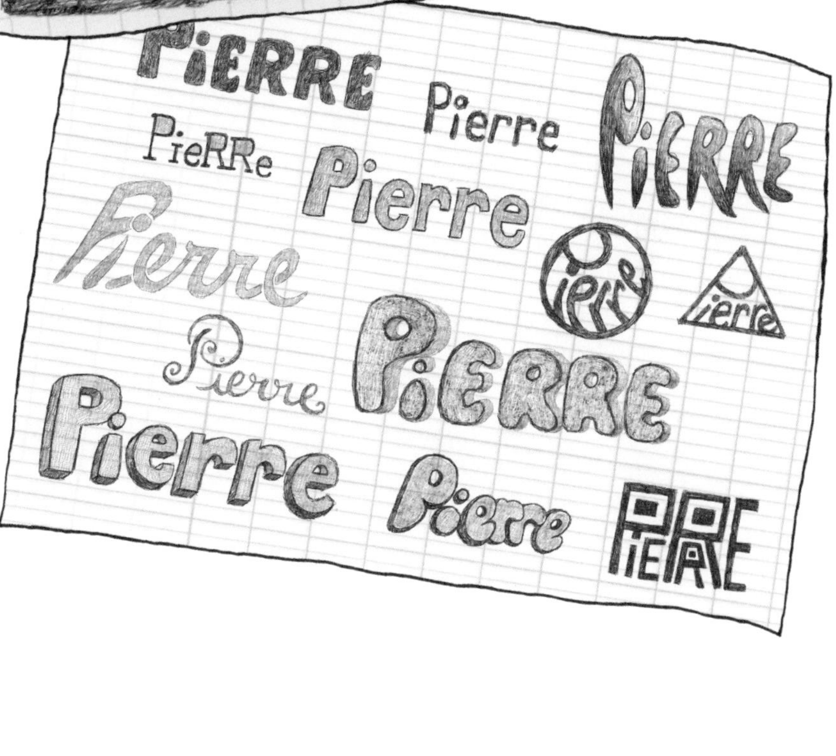
PIERRE
Pierre
PIERRE
PieRRe
Pierre
Pierre
Pierre
Pierre
Pierre
PIERRE
Pierre
Pierre
PIERRE

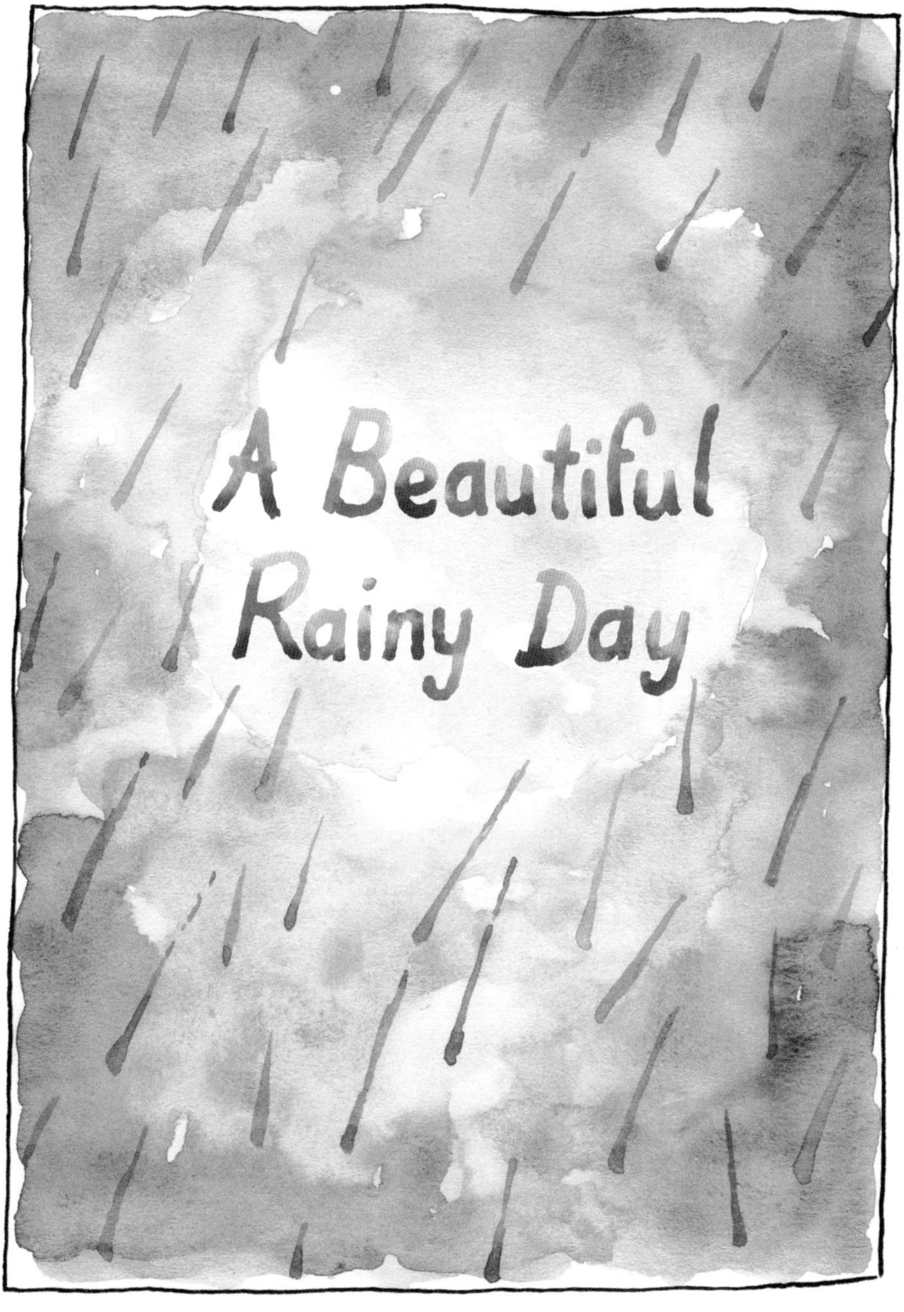
A Beautiful
Rainy Day

More than anything, Pierre and I were enjoying
spending time together.

Lyon was no more than an hour away,
but I had only been there to visit family friends
with my parents.

It was the first time I took the train
without my parents.

Au Sandwich Tunisien

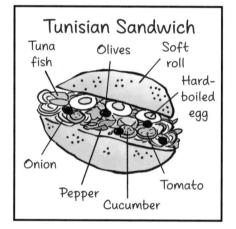

Tunisian Sandwich

Tuna fish

Olives

Soft roll

Hard-boiled egg

Onion

Pepper

Cucumber

Tomato

EAU*

*Water

We saw a movie.

*A Purple Taxi

The film was set in beautiful Ireland.

The story was packed with complicated relationships.

Reality felt a lot simpler. And wonderful!

When we got out of the theater, it was raining.
But we didn't mind.

I'll show you
the Old City.

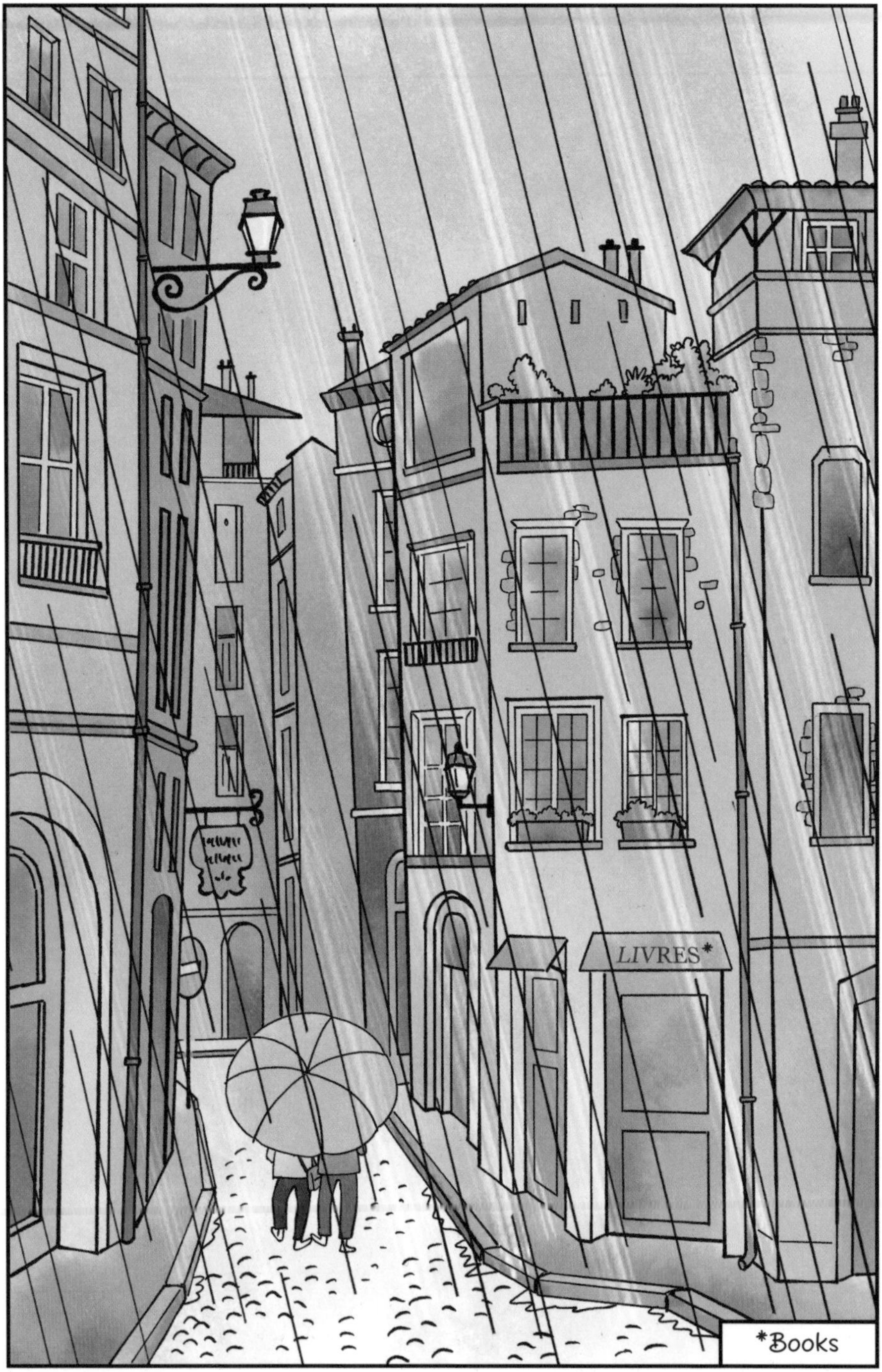
LIVRES*
*Books

Let's sit here
for a bit.

*Keep off grass

Pelouse
Interdite*

It had been a wonderful day. Yet I had been ignoring a troubling thought. I couldn't keep silent any longer.

It seemed so simple suddenly!
I felt at peace. My secret,
now shared, felt so much lighter.

On the ride back home, I leaned my head on
Pierre's shoulder.

I didn't move the whole ride.
Pierre didn't either.

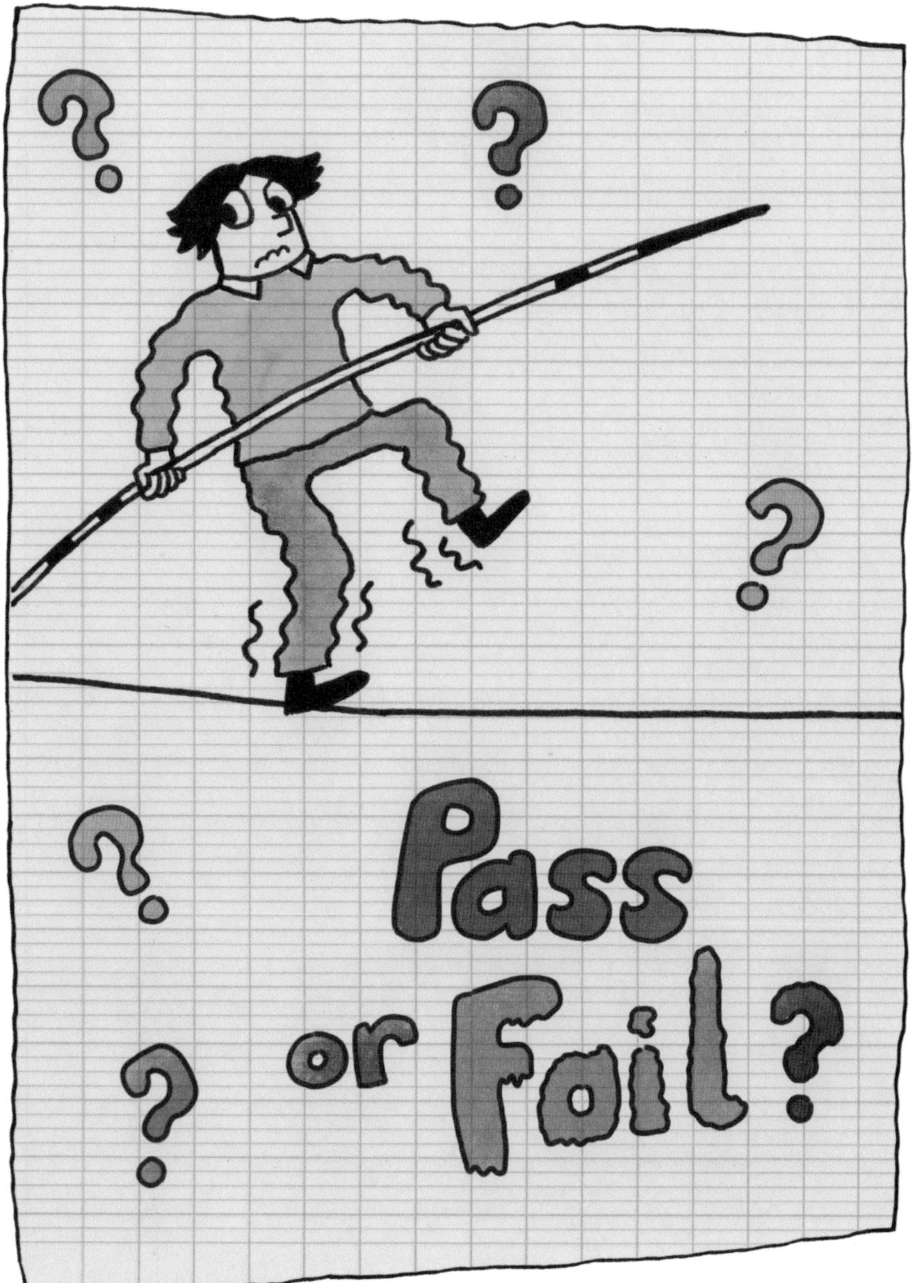
Pass or Fail?

All through high school, the focus was
the baccalaureate.

The bac diploma was the entrance ticket
to a university.

Passing would already be great! But passing with
honors, even an AB, would be such a source of pride!

HONORS		
TB	Très Bien	Very Good
B	Bien	Good
AB	Assez Bien	Fairly Good

At home, expectations were high.

Your cousin Mimi got a B.

It would be good if you got a TB.

Mom! I'm not even sure I'll pass!

At least a B, then.

Failing was out of the question.

Failing is for losers!

But what if I do fail?

At the start of high school, each student had had to make a choice among the sections offered by our school.

Section A focused on philosophy and literature. Section C was math and physics, and section D math and biology.

Apparently I was the only one thinking this choice an obvious one.

This was before Christine had left.

I'm definitely going for C.

All right, C for me too.

For three years, my world revolved around

math,

sigh

physics,

Yikes

and chemistry.

Aaaargh

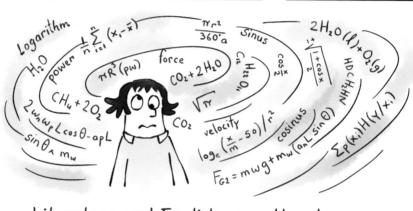

Literature and English were the classes
where I did well . . .

"Molière's use of
humor in *Don Juan*."
Very good essay,
Sylvie.

Good translation,
Sylvie. But
remember: no
future tense
after "when."

but they wouldn't count as much
in the final grade tally.

At one point, I had considered switching sections.

So I stuck with C.
And that was that.

The final exams were fast approaching.

It was all studying, reviewing, memorizing.

With Pierre constantly on my mind, it was hard to concentrate.

One evening, my world was turned upside down.

I actually stopped studying for a couple of days.

And it dawned on me how childish that was.

We spent a whole afternoon
on the velocity chapter.

And then the finals were upon us.

These days of intense testing were filled with dread and anxiety. Except for the art final! I was so glad I had chosen art as my elective option!

I saw students starting careful renderings in pencil.

I have something different in mind.

I felt good about my work.

You still have a little time left.

Thanks, but I'm done!

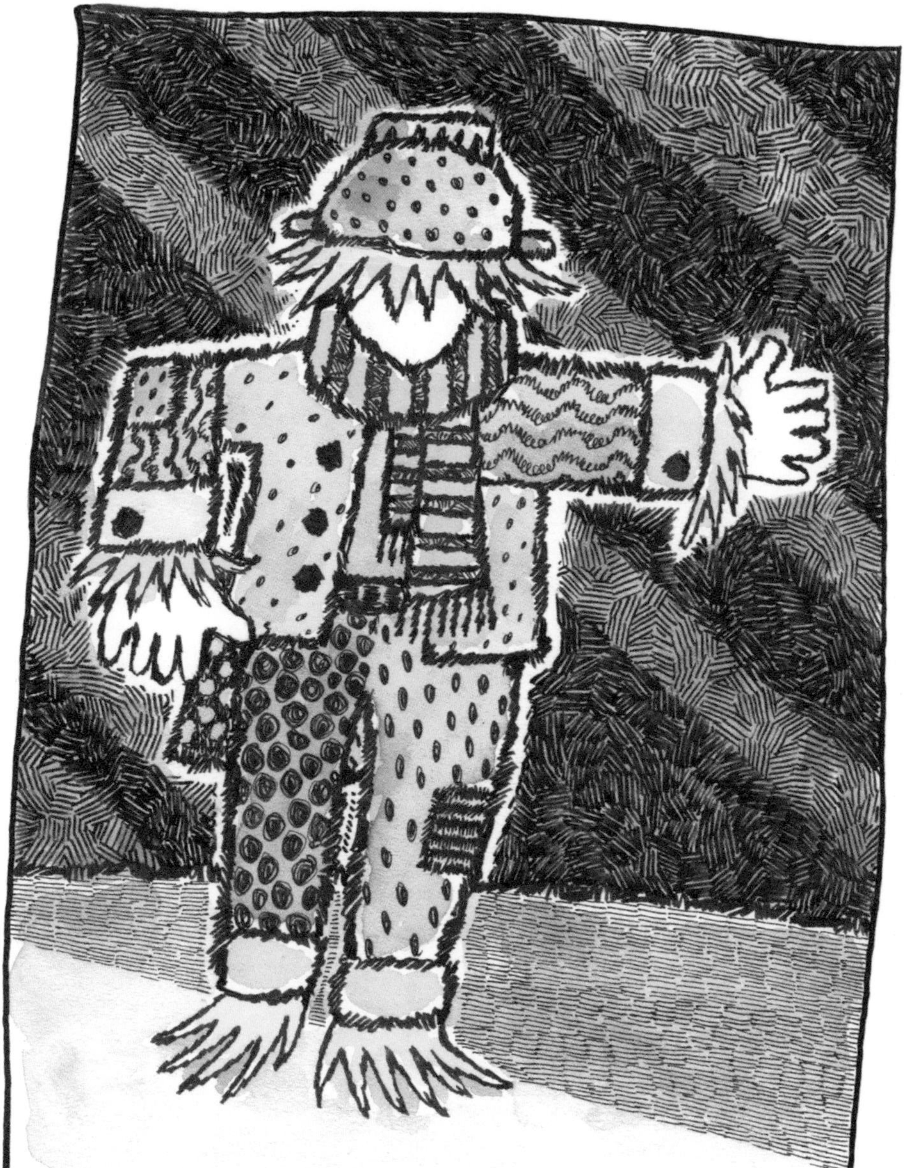

Not so happy was the physics final, in spite
of a hopeful start.

I dutifully reviewed the
numbers and returned
my paper.

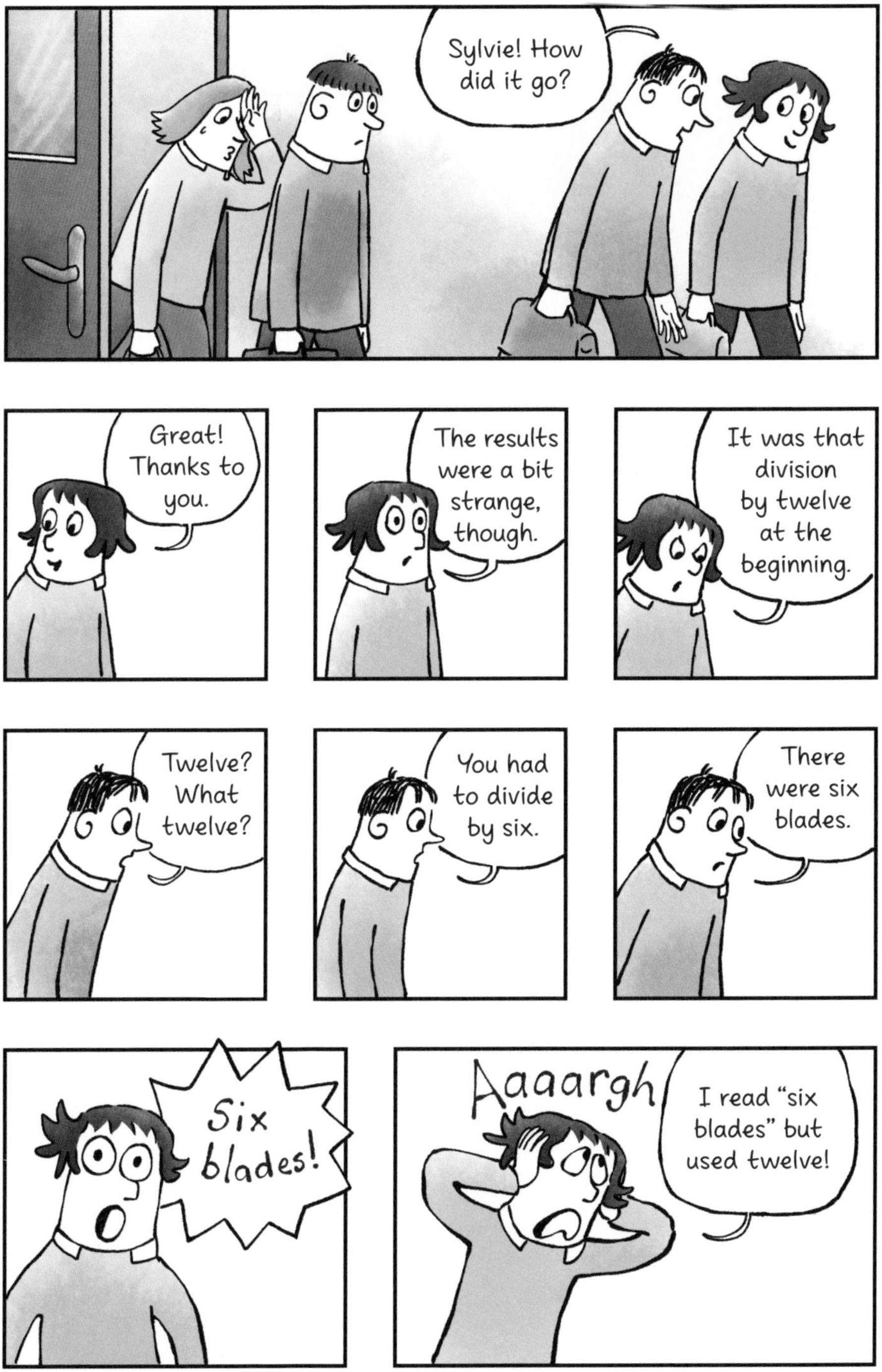
Sylvie! How did it go?
Great! Thanks to you.
The results were a bit strange, though.
It was that division by twelve at the beginning.
Twelve? What twelve?
You had to divide by six.
There were six blades.
Six blades!
Aaaargh
I read "six blades" but used twelve!

Why? Why?

How dumb can I be?

No wonder my results looked off.

A poor grade in physics would bring my average way down.

No way I'll pass now.

Waiting for the results, I tormented myself with endless speculations.

The day of the results came. The school posted the list of students who had passed.

My name _was_ on the list! How did I miss it?

Murle Jobert	section A	B
Daniel Justin	section D	pass
Sylvie Kantorovitz	section C	AB
Philippe Klotara	section A	pass
Jean-Michel Larmand	section C	pass

I made it!

I MADE IT!

I MADE IT!

And you?

Of course he had. Pierre was one of the best students in the whole school.

Yes, me too.

My parents were pleased.

Mom made her signature apple tart to celebrate.

Oh sure, there was an occasional nagging self-reproach.

But mostly I felt relieved.

Passing the bac seemed a good moment to ask for a much coveted haircut.

Reactions to the new haircut were mostly positive.

You look lovely, Sylvette.

You would look more feminine with a little makeup.

Mom, you know I hate makeup.

Mom did treat me to a pendant and matching earrings. I loved them!

I think she looks like a boy.

Pfffff

Suddenly, life was taking new turns.

I had been so focused on the bac, I had blocked out thoughts about my future studies.

Writing letters seemed very romantic.

Being apart didn't seem quite so bad anymore.

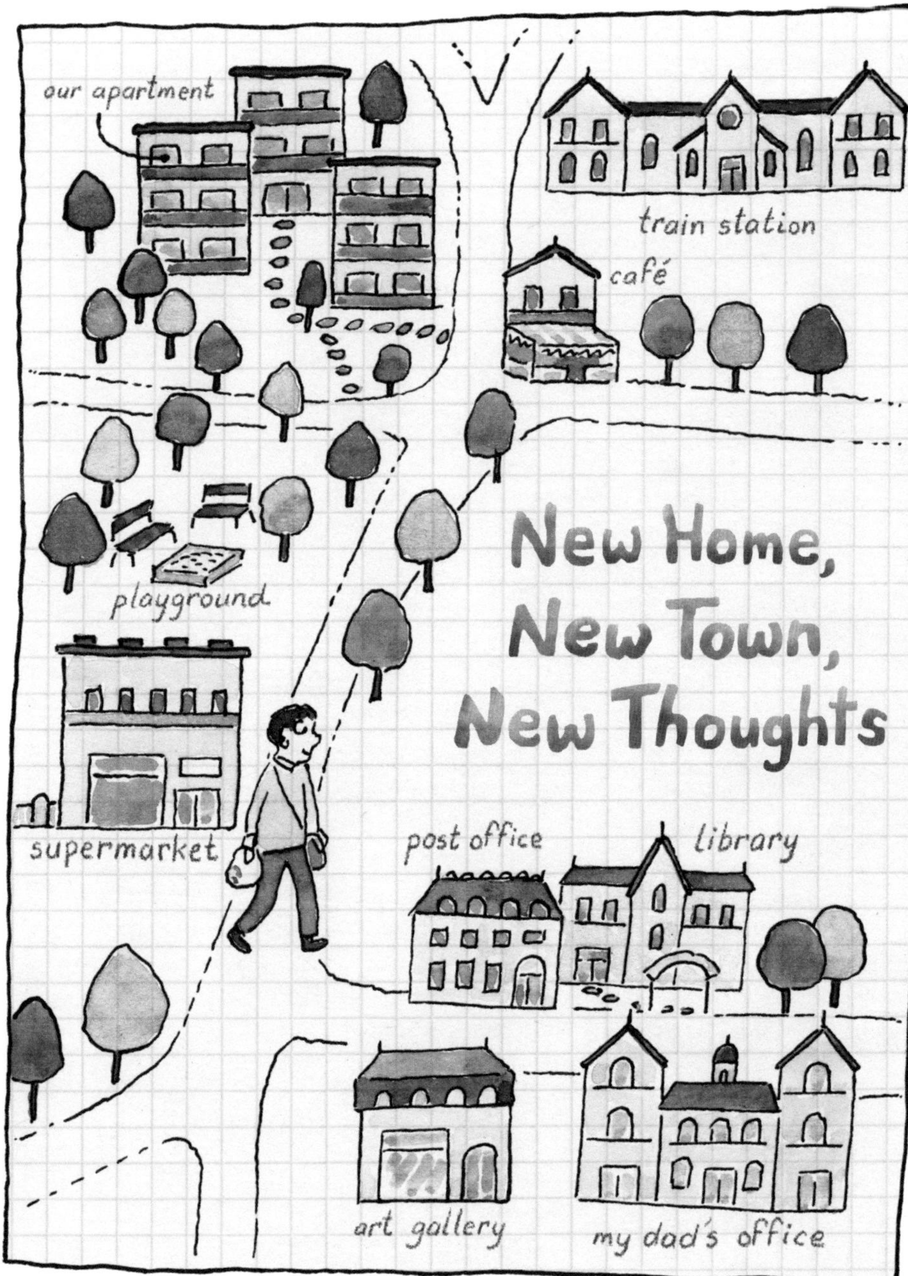
our apartment
train station
café
New Home,
New Town,
New Thoughts
playground
supermarket
post office
library
art gallery
my dad's office

Soon it was time to pack for the move.

I had outgrown so many things. Some were hard to let go. Some not at all!

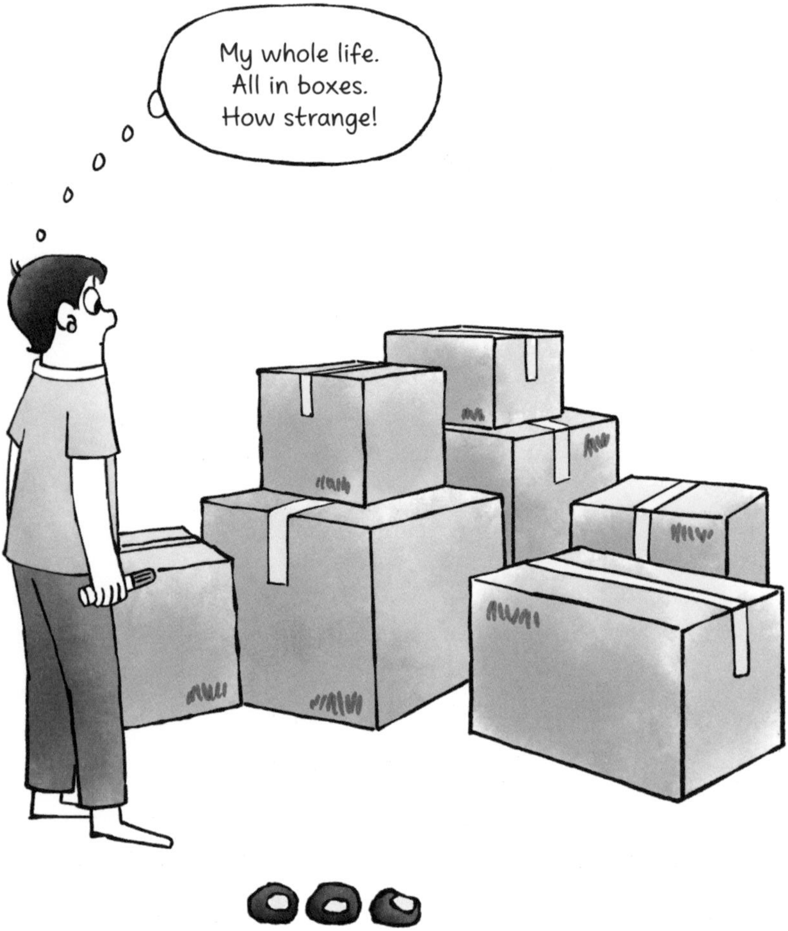
My whole life. All in boxes. How strange!

Dad and I were to leave for our new town
a week before the others.

I said goodbye to my attic room . . .

and got ready to leave my home-in-a-school. Forever.

The hardest part was saying goodbye to Pierre.

That's it. We are leaving tomorrow.

Look! I have something for you.

How pretty!

He also had a card. That he had drawn himself!

Thank you, Pierre.

Dad and I left early the next morning.

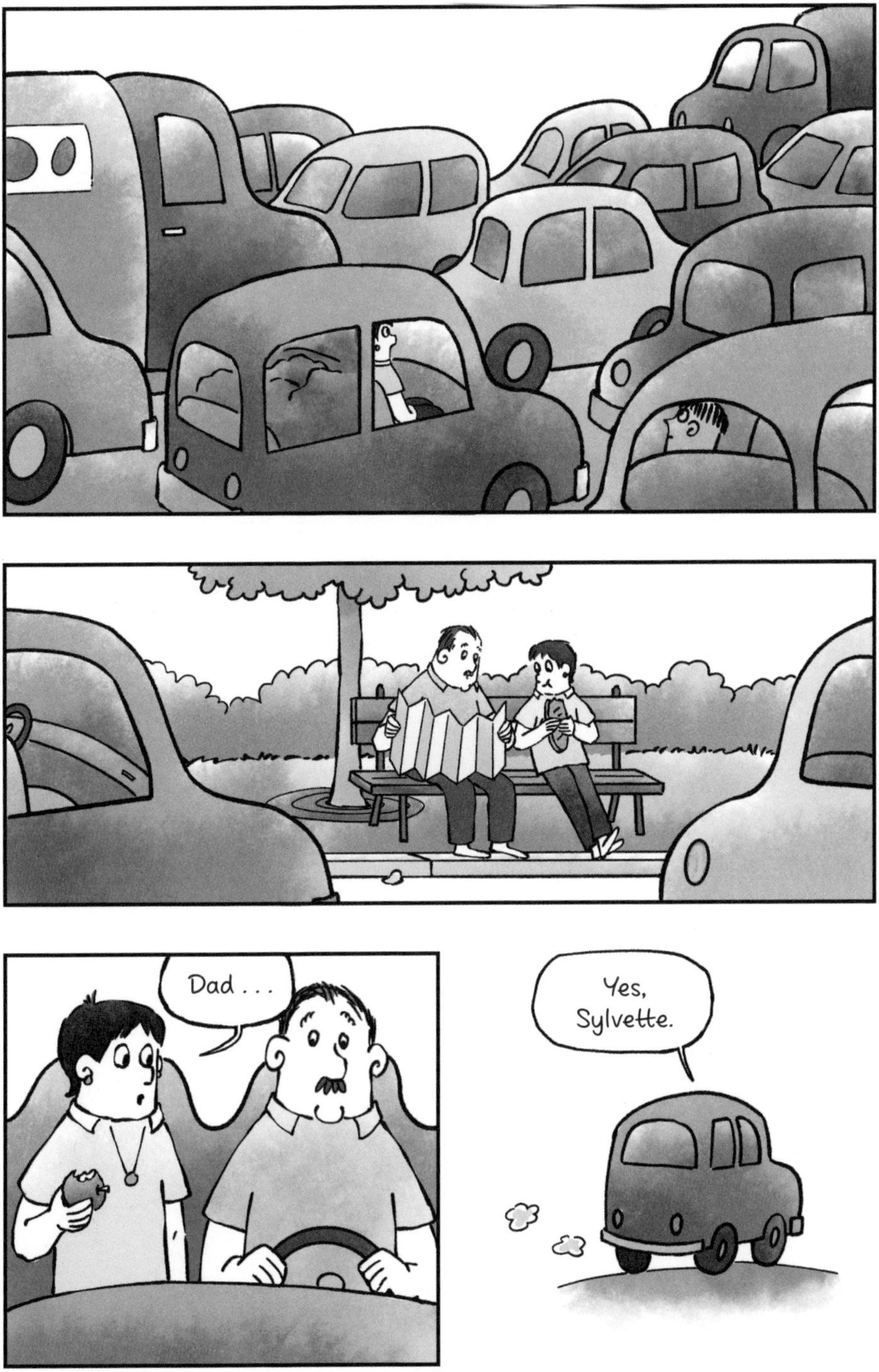
Dad . . .
Yes, Sylvette.

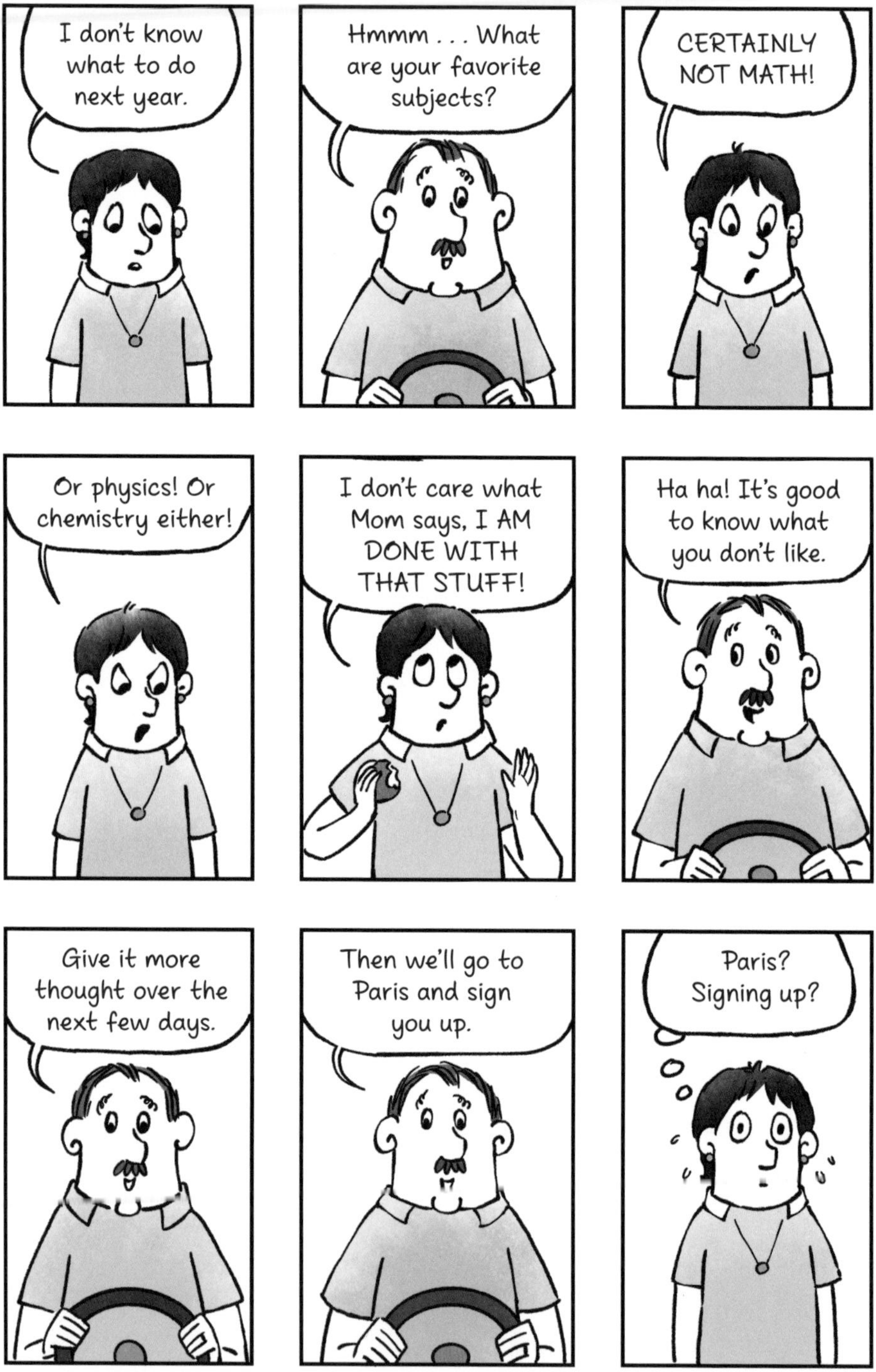
I don't know what to do next year.
Hmmm . . . What are your favorite subjects?
CERTAINLY NOT MATH!
Or physics! Or chemistry either!
I don't care what Mom says, I AM DONE WITH THAT STUFF!
Ha ha! It's good to know what you don't like.
Give it more thought over the next few days.
Then we'll go to Paris and sign you up.
Paris? Signing up?

Dad seems so casual about this . . .

So it's OK if I don't pick math?

The bac C allowed you to have more options . . .

But it's time for you to make your own choices.

I loved my student years in Paris!

I think you will too.

When I went back to Morocco, I was proud of my teaching diploma.

WOW!

The new apartment was in a modern building.

Welcome to our new abode, mademoiselle.

The moving van was not due for a while. Till then,
our camping stuff came in handy.

The next few days, Dad had to work, so I set out
to discover our new town.

BOULANGERIE - PÂTISSERIE*

*Bread and cake shop

I'll bring the little ones here; they will love it.

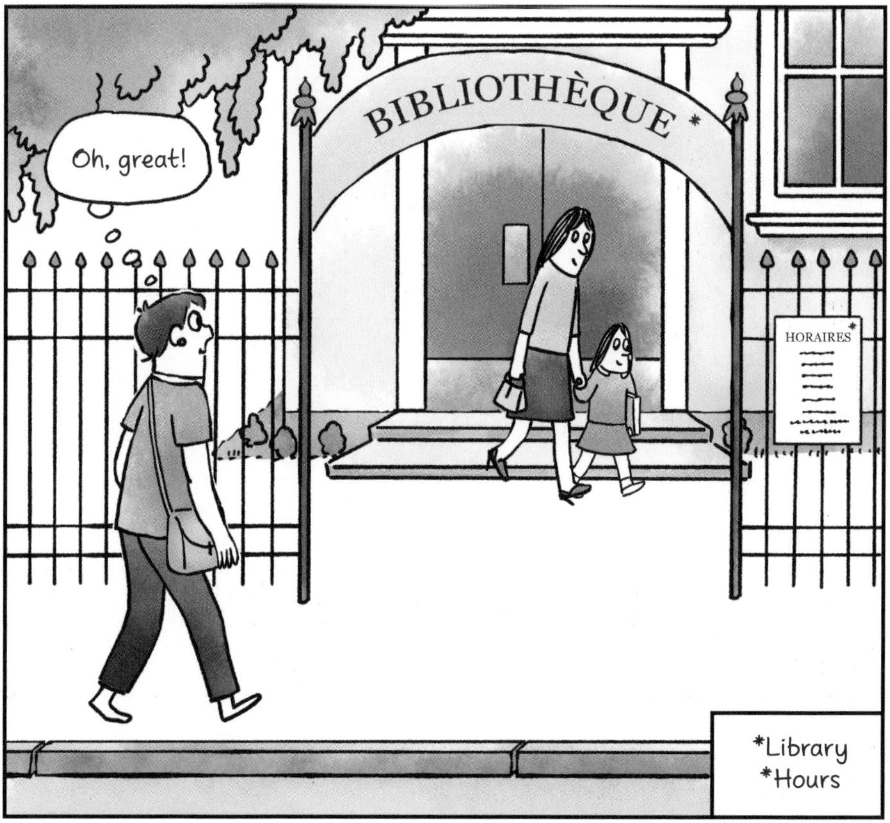
Oh, great!
BIBLIOTHÈQUE*
HORAIRES*
*Library
*Hours

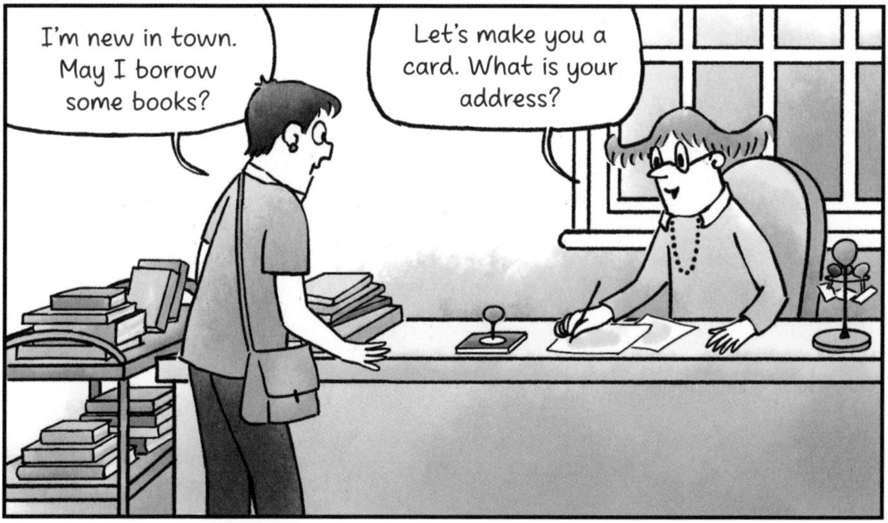
I'm new in town. May I borrow some books?
Let's make you a card. What is your address?

Later, I also stopped by the train station . . .

and picked up a schedule.

So many trains to Paris!

Wow! The trip doesn't even take that long!

Dad had put me in charge of groceries.

First, pasta.

I know Mom likes this brand of olive oil.

A Camembert, a piece of Comté, some Roquefort, and yum! A Caprice des Dieux.

various cheeses

Lettuce. And some peaches for dessert.

All set!

Delicious little dinner, Sylvette.

It was so nice here with just Dad. So quiet.

Dad . . . Mom gets angry at you so often.

Yes, Sylvette . . . I'm sorry.

Mom will be happier here.

Was it possible? Could one stay in love in spite of so much arguing?

One evening, there was a letter from Pierre.

Maybe you can come
and visit during
winter break.
My parents are OK
with it. Ask your
parents.
It would be so nice
and we could go

I was missing Pierre so much.
I read that letter over and over.

One afternoon, I met some neighbors.

What grade are you in, Sylvie?

I just passed the bac.

I will be studying in Paris in the fall.

What will you study?

I'm not sure yet. But I will decide soon!

Say, Sylvie, do you babysit?

I often take care of my little sister and brother.

Could you take care of Colin tomorrow morning?

I'd love to!

Babysitting was fun! Just like taking care of the little ones. But now I was being paid!

Am, stram, gram, pic et pic et colégram*...

*Eenie, meenie, miney, mo . . .

Wow! Very good circle.

Look, Colin. A camel.

Hello! I'm home!

Look, Mommy!

It's beautiful, Colin!

Thank you, Sylvie. I'll call you again soon.

Would teaching feel like that?

That afternoon, I passed an art gallery.

* The Art Cavern

On a whim, I went in.

How beautiful!

I would love to have one of these!

Maybe one day . . .

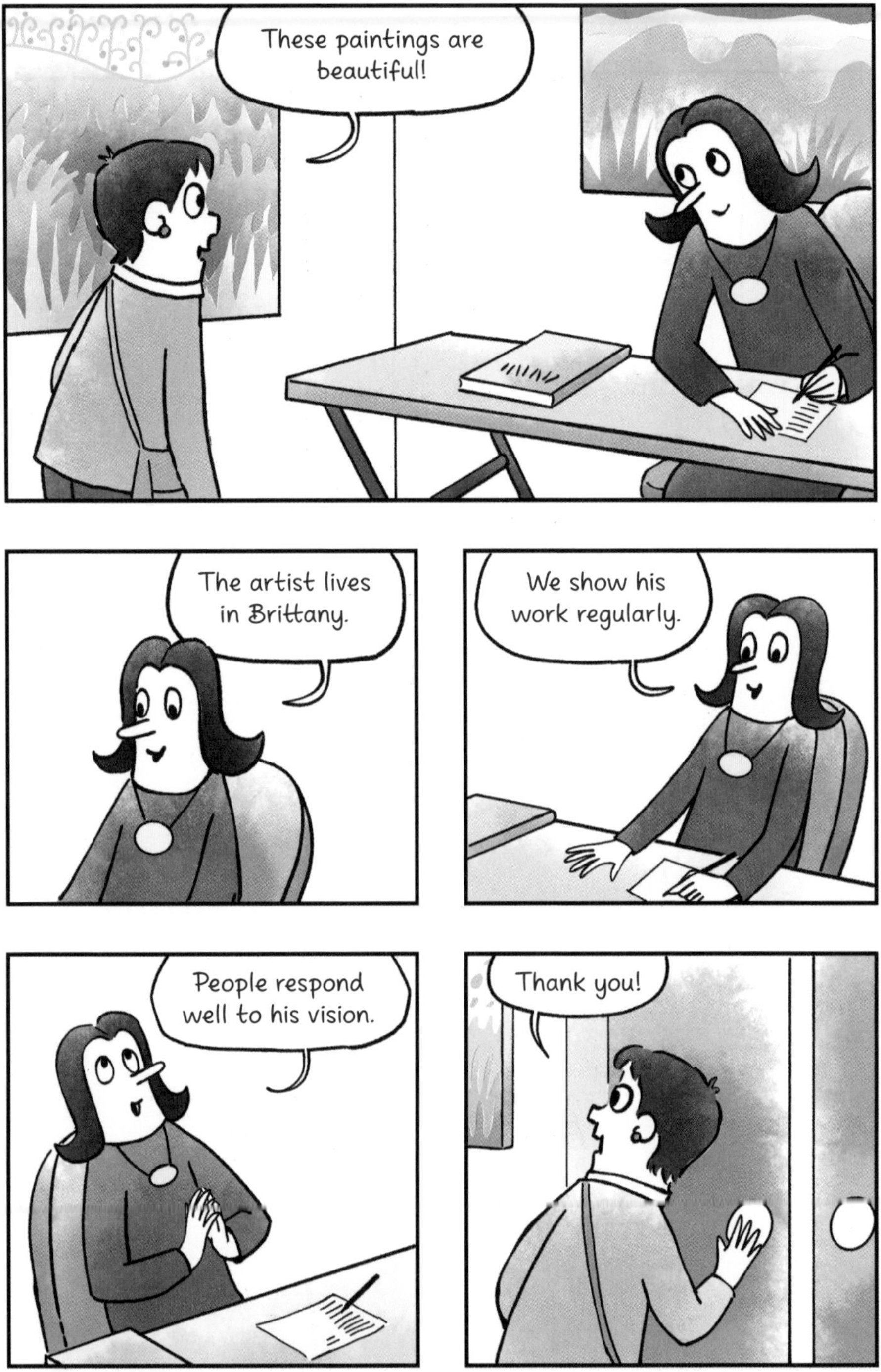
These paintings are beautiful!
The artist lives in Brittany.
We show his work regularly.
People respond well to his vision.
Thank you!

I went back to the library to get my new card
and take out some books.

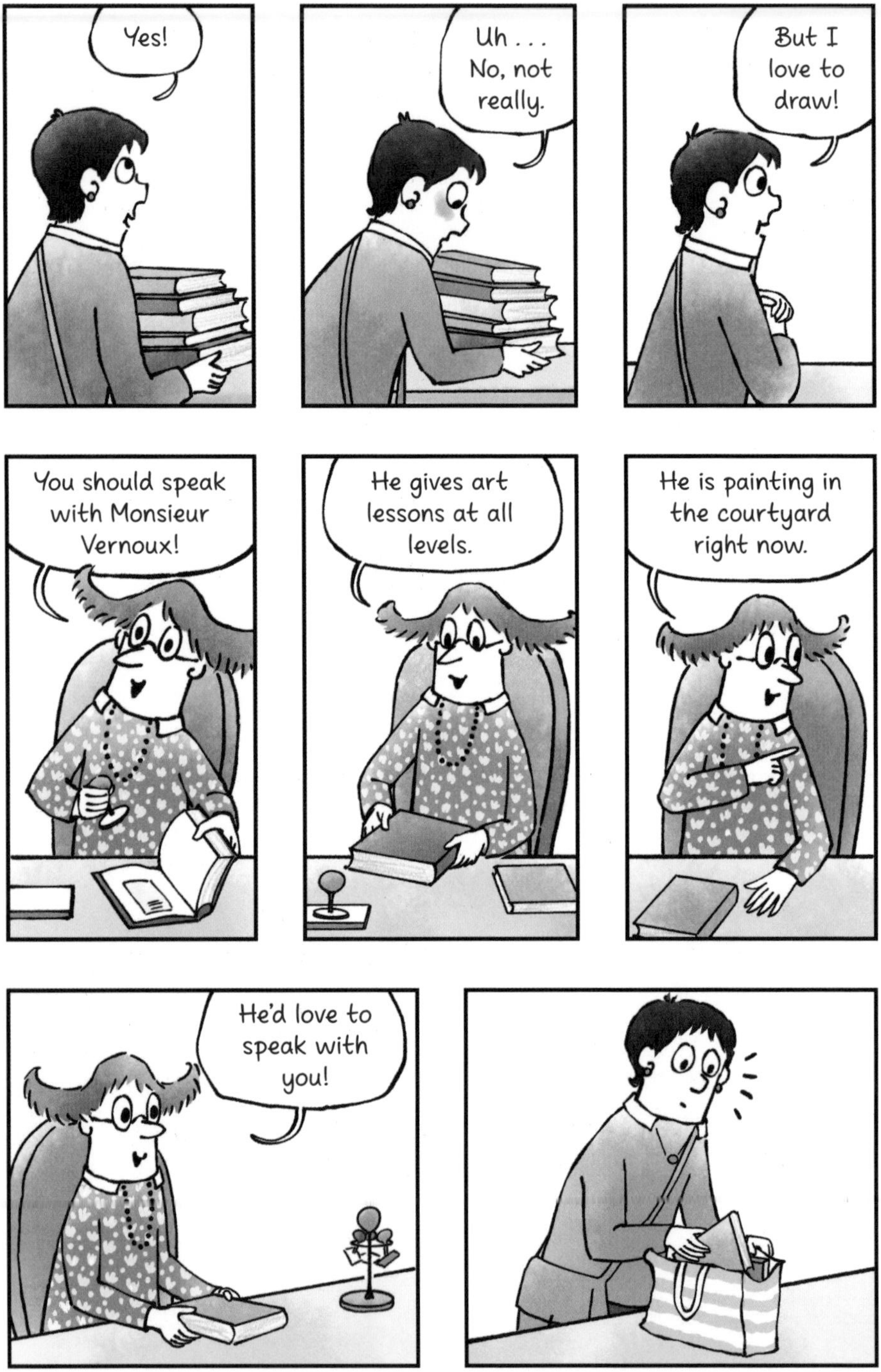
Yes!
Uh . . . No, not really.
But I love to draw!
You should speak with Monsieur Vernoux!
He gives art lessons at all levels.
He is painting in the courtyard right now.
He'd love to speak with you!

Wow! This is so good!

Thank you!

Excuse me. The librarian said you give art lessons. . . .

Monsieur Vernoux took a break.

I had never even imagined pursuing any kind of art studies. But the minute he suggested just that, the notion gripped my mind and wouldn't let go!

With Dad at work, I had plenty of thinking time.

Some people make a living as artists.

I could be one of them.

I don't need a lot of money!

Still, I need to make enough to live on.

I cannot depend on my parents forever!

Teaching would be a good job.

But I would miss art so much!

One minute I was sure I wanted to be an artist. The next one, I knew it was foolish. I just couldn't make up my mind.

When the rest of the family arrived,
I was still undecided.

So, Sylvette, have you thought about next year?

How about commercial studies?

I heard it's the best option for girls with a bac C.

Certainly not!

Mom, please, I need a little more time to think.

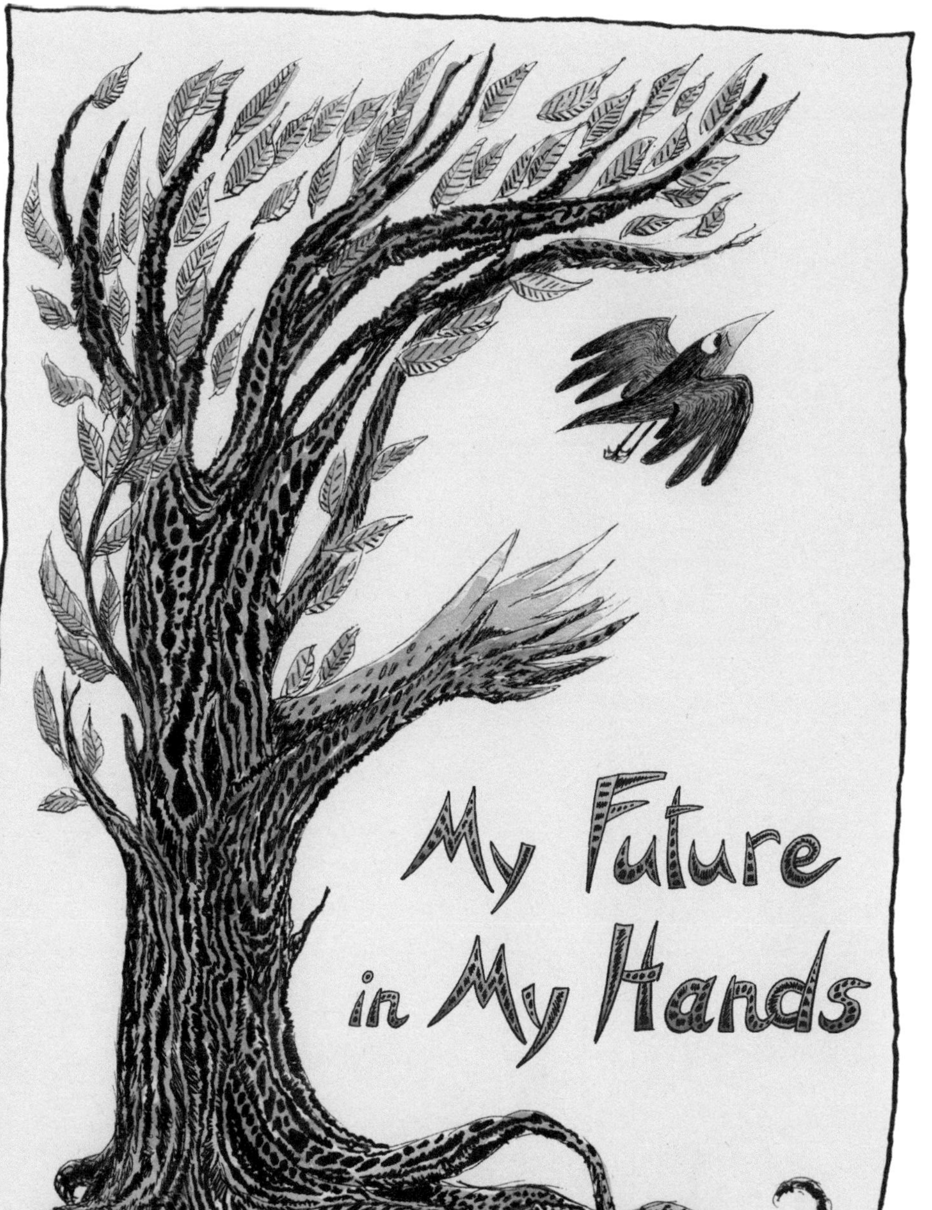
My Future
in My Hands

So, what were my choices?

I definitely liked
young children.

Teaching little ones sounded quite appealing.
But what about drawing?

I love to
draw.

But it WOULD
be a risky choice!

What if I can't
make a living
at it?

I need to find out more about teaching school!

I knew talking with Mom would be pointless. Conversations with her often left me completely baffled!

You are pretty enough to attract a rich husband.

MOM!

I'm not looking for a husband!

You could do pharmacy. . . .

Meet a nice Jewish pharmacy student!

But . . . I like Pierre!

Oh, Pierre is just a crush!

Besides . . . he is not very generous.

What did Mom expect from a seventeen-year-old boy? Furs? Diamonds?

I needed to talk with my dad! I went to see him at his office.

Dad, I have some questions about teaching school.

He provided all the info I needed.

You can become a teacher in three years.

Two years of study and one of practice.

You could start making an income soon.

And have plenty of free time for drawing....

wink

Dad, was it hard for you to decide what you wanted to do after high school?

You know how different it was for me, Sylvette.

Growing up in Morocco! We were so poor, I left home at fourteen...

jumping at the chance to enroll in a special program offered by the French government.

They would pay for my studies, including teaching school in Paris. In exchange, I would teach for a minimum of ten years.

So . . . you were stuck teaching?

The thing is, I really like teaching. So I never felt stuck.

In fact, I felt very fortunate!

I was even able to send some money to my family in Morocco.

Besides . . .

That's how I met Mom! She was in the same program, you know.

Mom wants me to marry a rich man!

I hate it when she says things like that!

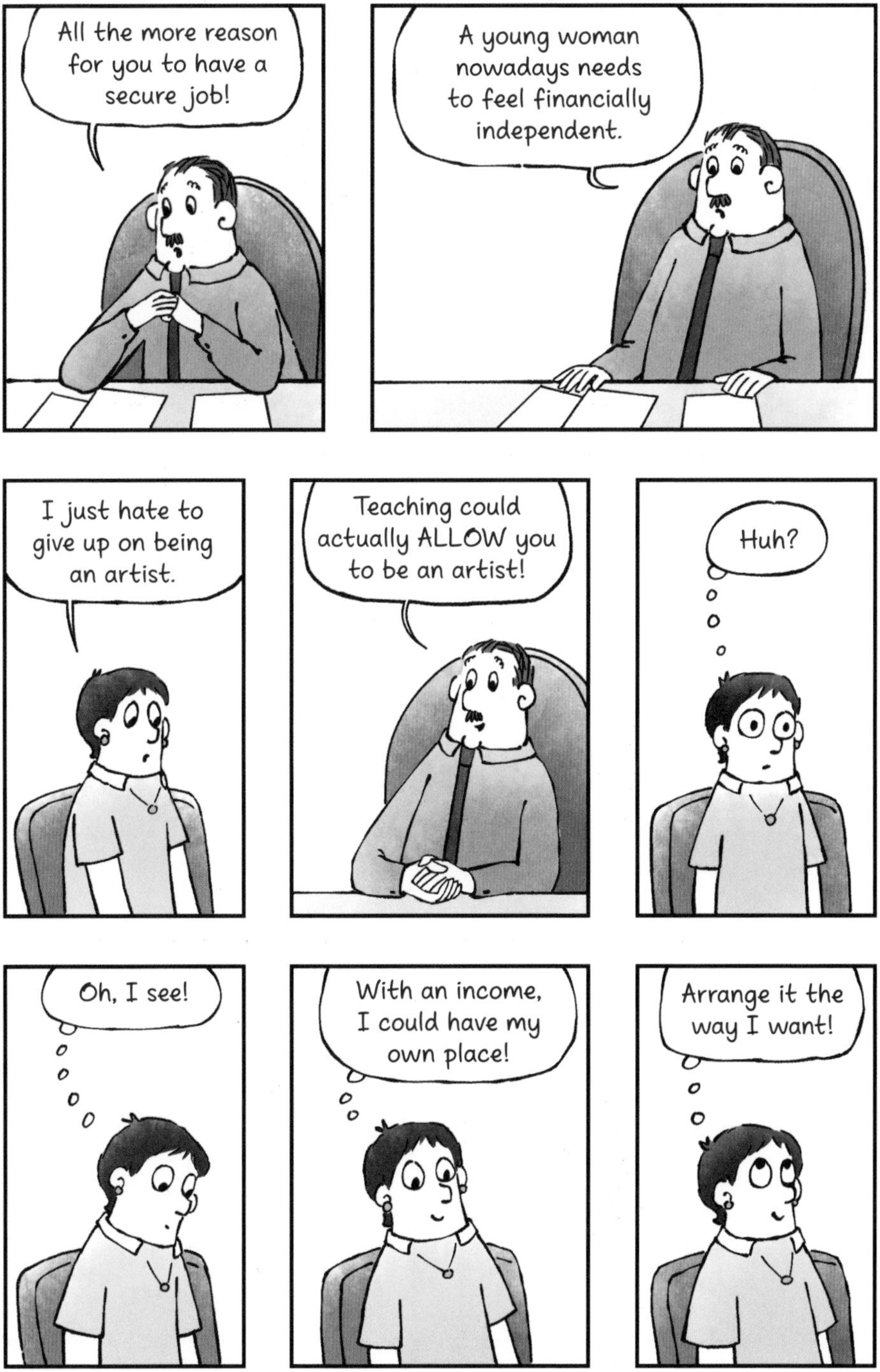
All the more reason for you to have a secure job!
A young woman nowadays needs to feel financially independent.
I just hate to give up on being an artist.
Teaching could actually ALLOW you to be an artist!
Huh?
Oh, I see!
With an income, I could have my own place!
Arrange it the way I want!

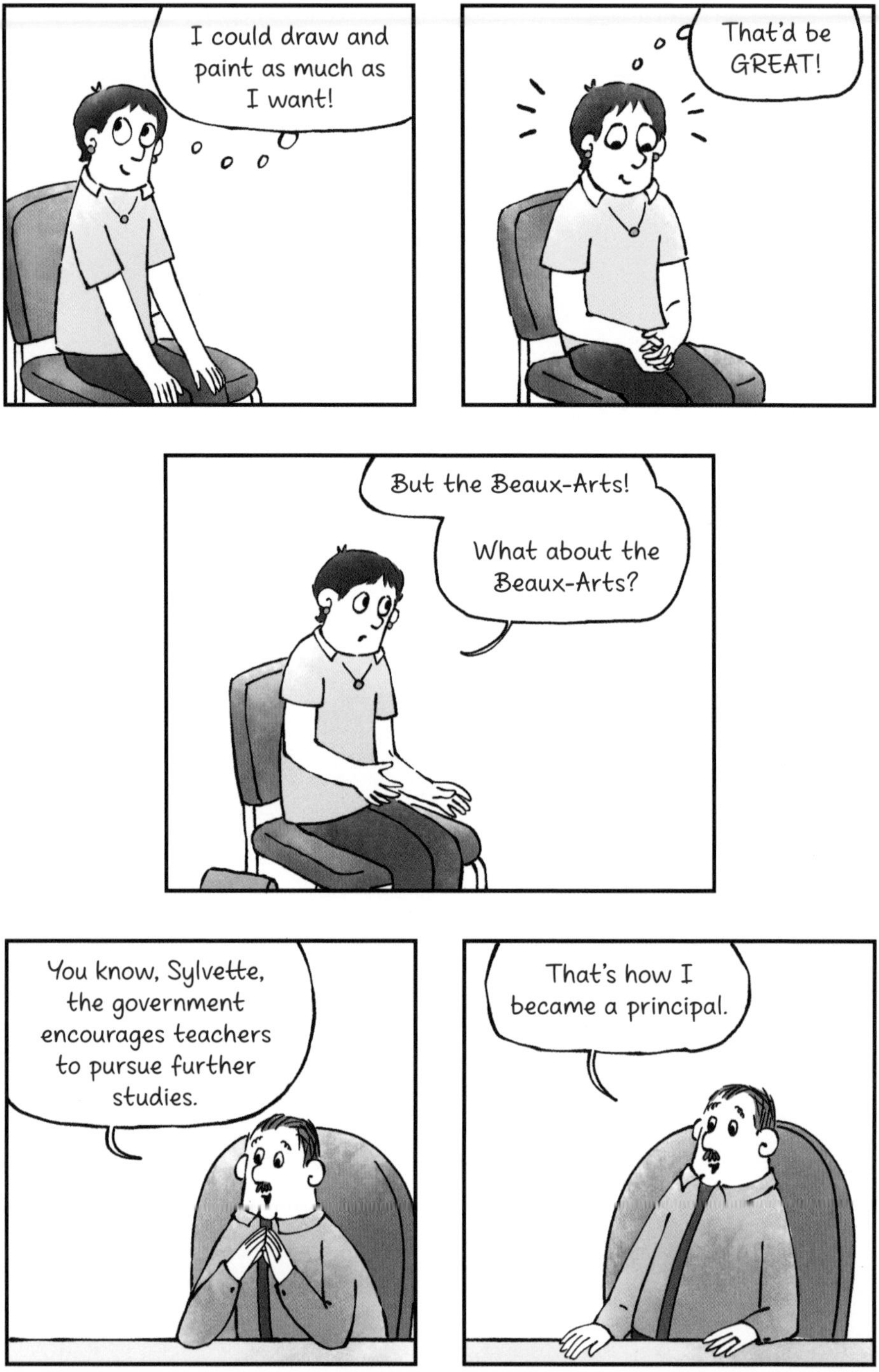
I could draw and paint as much as I want!
That'd be GREAT!
But the Beaux-Arts!
What about the Beaux-Arts?
You know, Sylvette, the government encourages teachers to pursue further studies.
That's how I became a principal.

I left my dad's office with new thoughts swirling in my head.

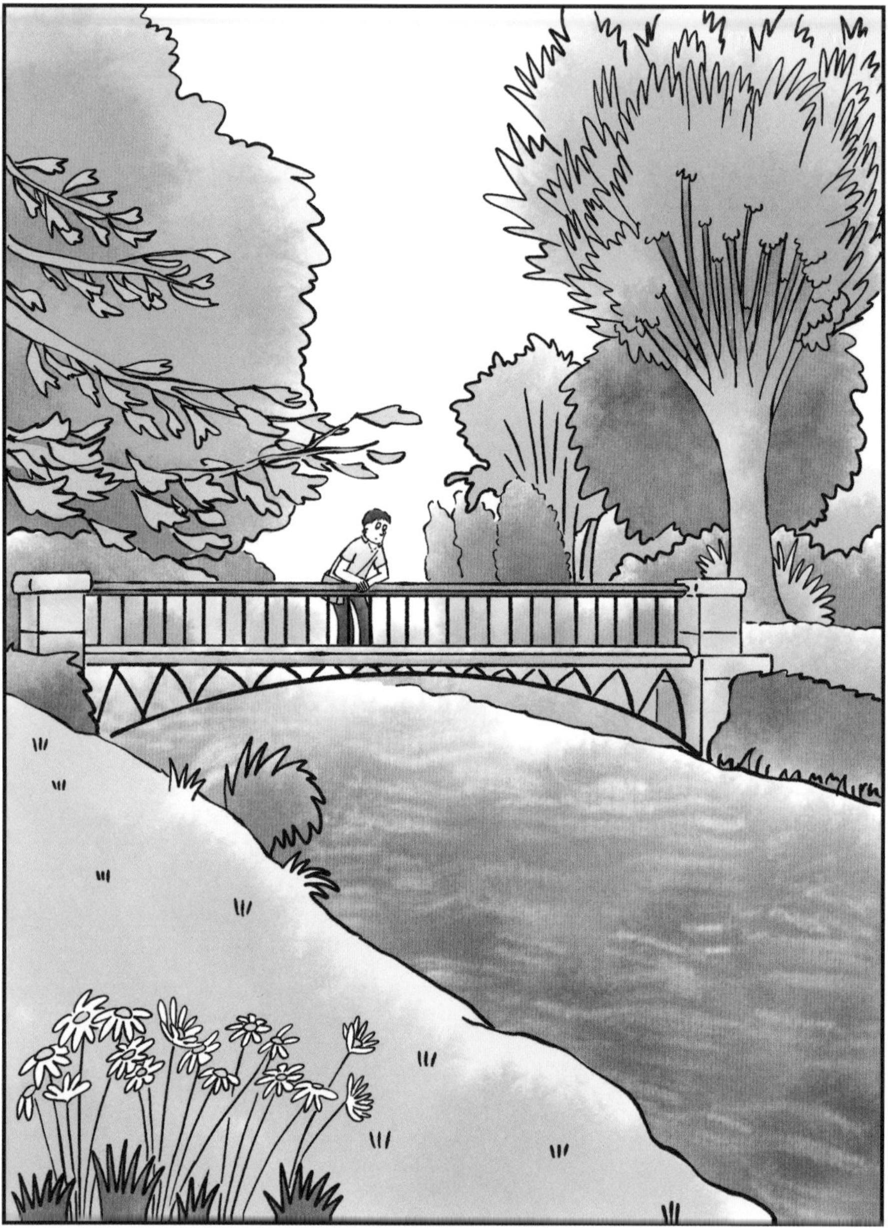

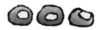

I went to see Monsieur Vernoux.
I wanted to hear his opinion.

Monsieur Vernoux, I will not be able to apply to the Beaux-Arts this fall.

I need to be more practical.

But I would like to apply in three years, after I've become a teacher.

Ha ha! That gives us plenty of time to get you ready!

I did something like that myself, you know.

Nothing wrong with a long-term plan!

A long-term plan!
Oh, I liked that!

Now that I had my own plan,
it was time to speak with Mom.

Mom switched gears:

I am NOT good at math!

I hate it!

I do not want to "bank on" anything!

I know you don't enjoy teaching.

But to ME, it would be meaningful!

I want to do something meaningful!

I don't want to work just for the money.

Well! If that's how you want to look at it . . .

As long as I was confronting Mom,
I might as well tell it all.

My plan is to apply to the Beaux-Arts after I get my teaching degree.

What can I do?

I've produced an artist!

And later . . .

Sylvie wants to teach! Just like me! She also wants to be an artist!

Yes . . . I have an idealistic daughter!

Well, if that's how _she_ wanted to look at it, it was fine with me!

sigh

Dad, of course, was happy with my decision.

I was eager to share my thoughts with Pierre.

Dear Pierre, I have so much to tell you

And now, after a summer full of preparations, I was on my way to my little student room in Paris. On my way to independence! Tomorrow would be my first day at teaching school.

And in my bag, I had an assignment from Monsieur Vernoux. I knew I would get it done before our next session.

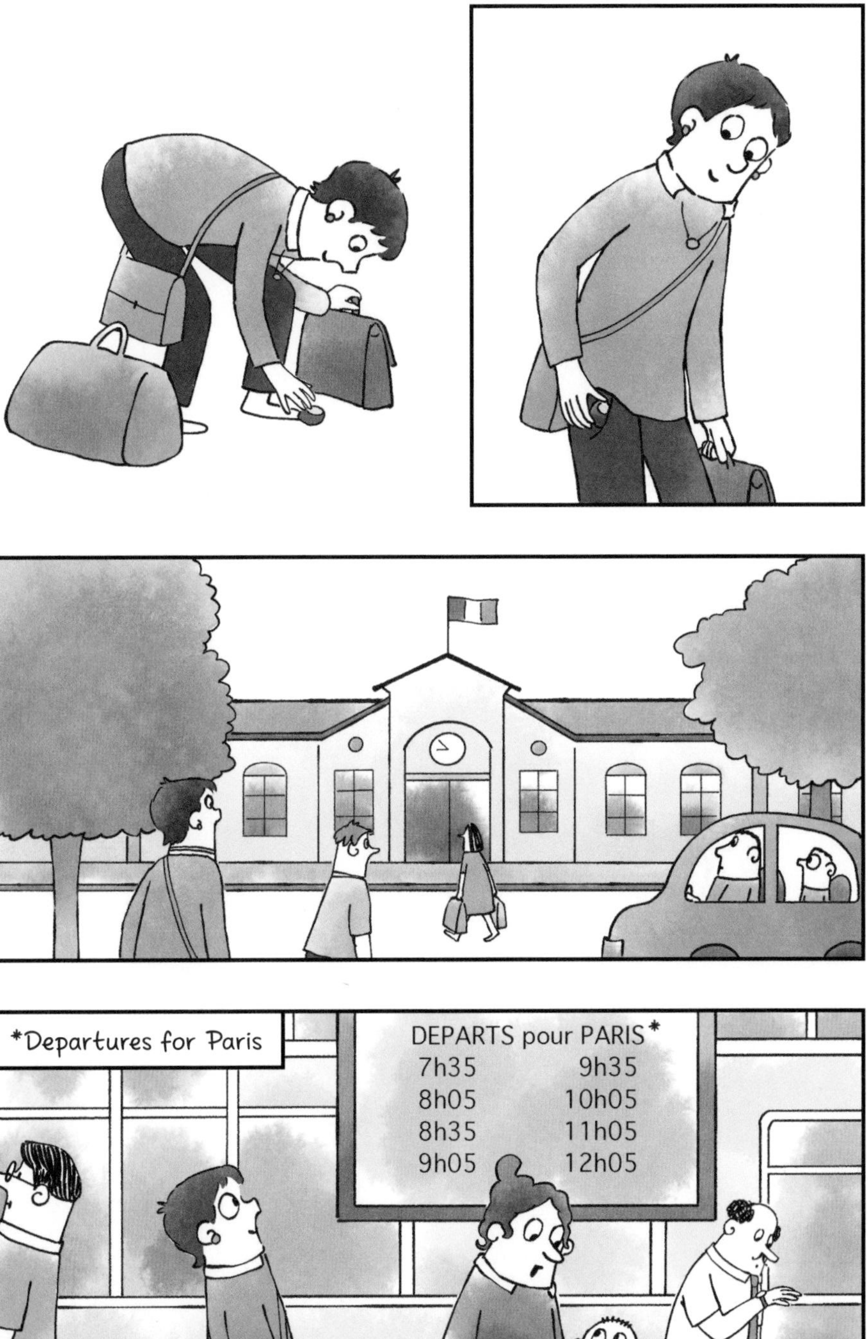
*Departures for Paris
DEPARTS pour PARIS*
7h35 9h35
8h05 10h05
8h35 11h05
9h05 12h05

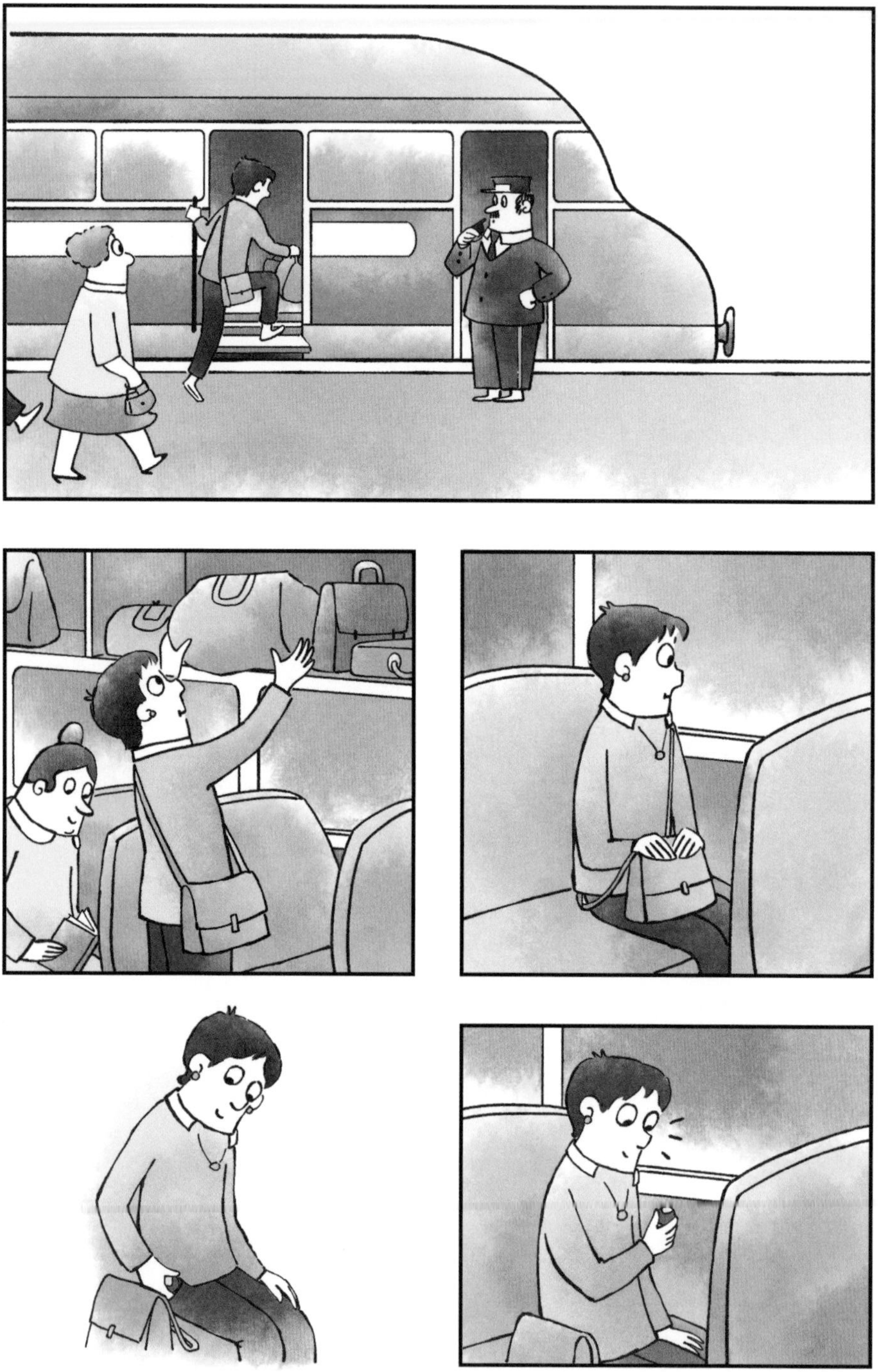

PARIS

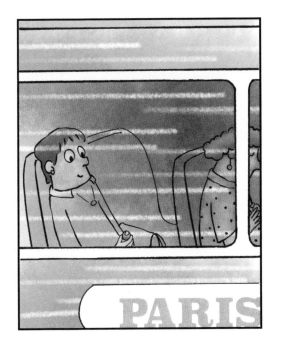

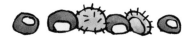

Author's Note

What a strange experience it is to write a memoir. To spend so much time delving into one's own beginnings!

However, I didn't set out to write a memoir. This is what I thought would happen: I'd write a book about a French girl, using anecdotes inspired from my childhood, when I lived in a school. When I couldn't remember something, I'd make it up!

This is what actually happened: At first my memories of exactly who, when, and how were a bit hazy. However, I remembered my feelings very clearly. These feelings triggered the memories of specific anecdotes, events, and conversations. As I progressed, memories kept resurfacing, one leading to another.

When I was missing details, I just imagined what I or the people in my life would have said or done, and—POOF!—there they were. Maybe not verbatim, maybe tweaked for the sake of a fluid narrative, but true nonetheless. Emotionally true!

Themes and threads emerged that I had not anticipated. In particular the relationship with my parents, the fear of being different, and the need to think for myself.

Without really intending to, I had written a memoir!

Writing about myself turned out to be an illuminating experience. I feel I know more about who I am than I did before I started. Someone long ago said "Know thyself." Whoever they were, they were right! Finding out who we are, and not who others think we are or want us to be, is the most important search in life.

Acknowledgments

Since my very first book, I have understood the importance of a good team working toward the best possible result. The team for *Sylvie* is top-notch!

Barbara read and read and read. Over and over! Page after page after page. And she provided the best encouragement one could ask for: "More, please!"

Rebecca saw potential and matched me with Susan.

Susan directed the shaping of raw material into a cohesive narrative.

Maria was there guiding my first foray into digital illustration.

Faye enthusiastically joined in.

Thank you all for your expertise, help, support, and kindness!

About the Author-Illustrator

Sylvie Kantorovitz was born in Casablanca and grew up in France. She is the author-illustrator of many picture books. This is her first work of graphic nonfiction. She lives in New York's Hudson Valley with her partner, Barbara Lehman, also an author-illustrator.

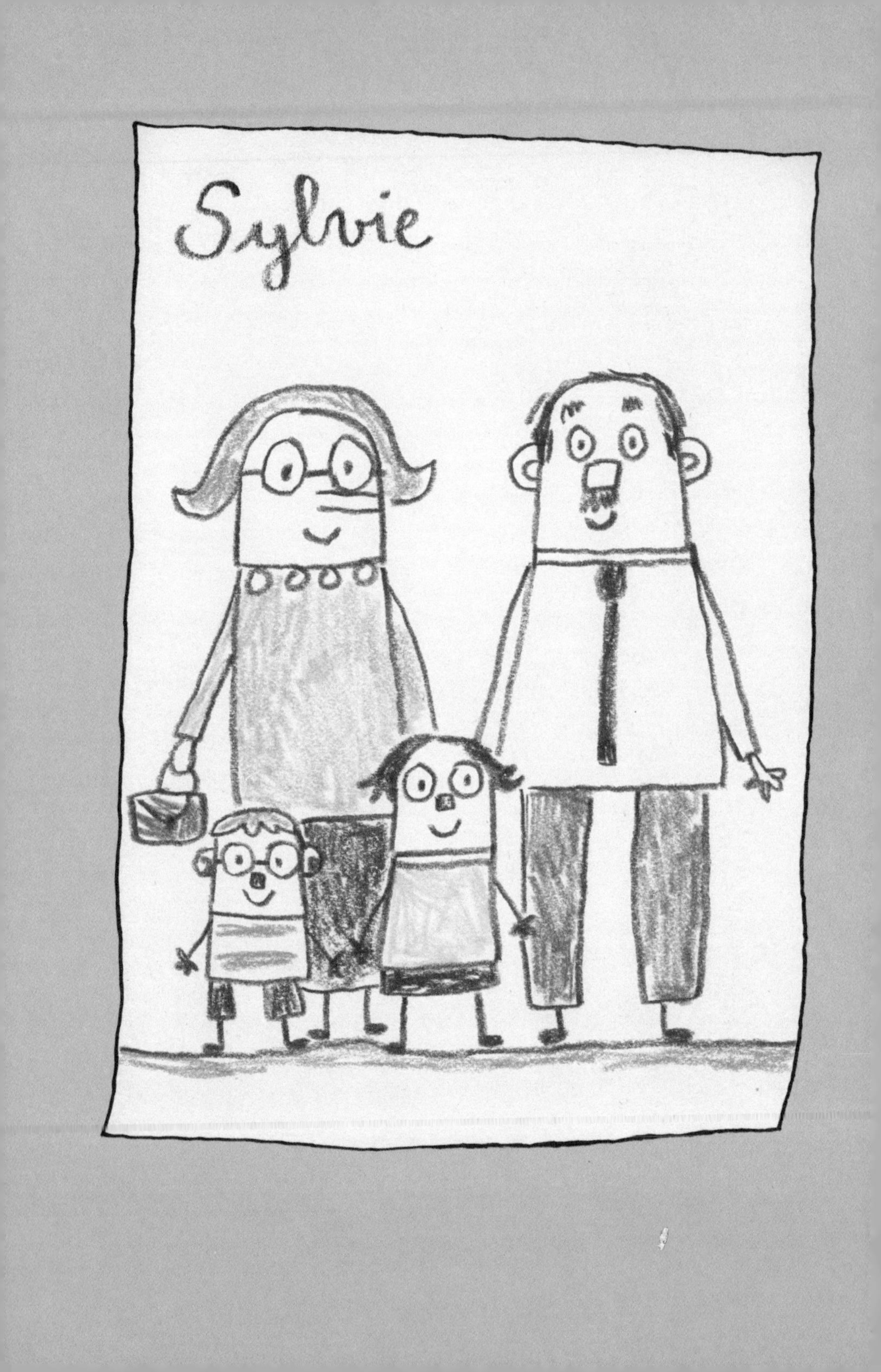
Sylvie

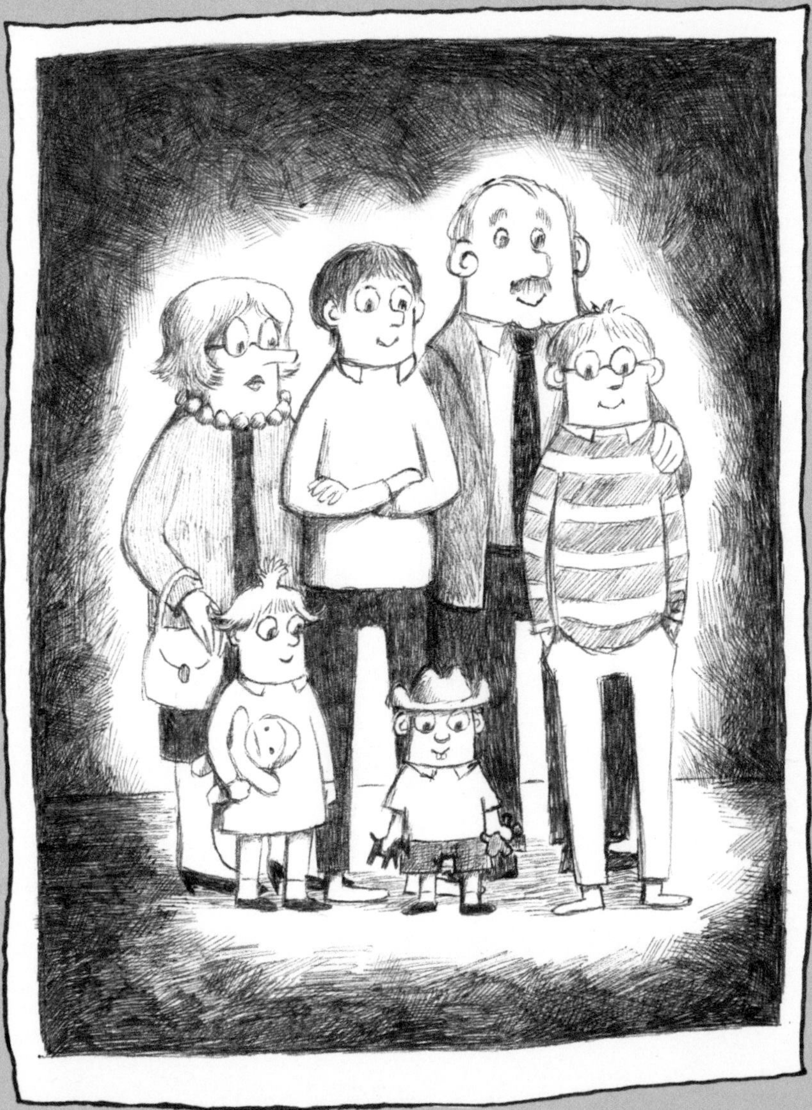